A story of music
from Bach to Puccini

CONTENTS

D0552564

Maxim Vengerov playing the Tchaikovsky Violin
Concerto for *Great Composers*

Introduction

Millions have watched and enjoyed BBC2's Great Composers, the first series of its kind on British Television. The programmes explored the life and work of seven composers who, uniquely, both mirrored and revolutionized the musical world in which they lived.

The purpose of the films was to tell, in an informative, enlightening and entertaining way, a story of how music developed over a period of two hundred years, using different composers from Bach to Puccini as sign-posts for musical change.

In the space of a one-hour documentary, it is not possible to include every detail necessary to set each composer in his social and historical context. Nor is it possible to pay tribute to more than a fraction of the extraordinary music that they each composed. We hope, however, that in these films we were able to give a sense of the worlds in which these composers lived and worked.

This booklet, which presents an engaging and accessible overview of the life and work of each of the composers featured in the programmes, shares the aim of the series: to enhance the viewer's enjoyment of their music. As for the music itself, do seek it out on recordings (the booklet includes a discography), radio and television. And if you missed any of the Great Composers films, Warner Vision has released a two-video boxed set of the whole series.

My thanks go to executive producer Kriss Rusmanis – Great Composers was for him a three-year labour of love which he has now extended by writing this illuminating booklet – and the very able team he assembled to make the television series. Thanks must also go to BBC Education Production for publishing *A Story of Music from Bach to Puccini* and to our co-producers, NVC Arts.

AVRIL MACRORY
Head of Classical Music, Television

Bach

and the Baroque

ALTHOUGH MUSIC existed for thousands of years before his time, the compositions of the great German composer J. S. Bach represent the beginning of our modern era. Today Bach occupies a pivotal place in the history of music, and the depth of his influence has been almost unequalled. His compositions offered a blueprint for composers and musicians in their understanding of the basic 'rules' of composing. His adventurous harmony – often dissonant – and his complex   musical structures enriched his music with a new dramatic, emotional and spiritual intensity which was immensely influential and which has never been surpassed.

Historically, Bach represents the height of the Baroque era in music. 'Baroque' is little more than a convenient label for a period generally

JOHANN SEBASTIAN BACH – MAJOR WORKS

Sacred choral music
Magnificat, D (1723)
St John Passion (1724)
St Matthew Passion (1725)
Christmas Oratorio (1734)
Mass, B (1749)

Over 200 church cantatas including:
No. 80, Ein feste Burg ist unser Gott
(c1744)
No. 140, Wachet auf (1731)

Sacred Songs and Motets including:
Jesu meine Freude (c1723)
Singet dem Herrn (1727)

Secular vocal music
Over 30 secular cantatas including:
'Coffee Cantata' (c1735)
'Peasant Cantata' (1742)

Orchestral music
Brandenburg Concertos nos. 1–6 (1721)
4 orchestral suites (1725–31)
Harpsichord concertos

Chamber music
6 sonatas and partitas for solo violin (1720)
6 suites for solo cello (c1720)
6 sonatas for violin and harpsichord (1723)
Musikalisches Opfer (Musical Offering,
1747)

Keyboard music
Chromatic Fantasia and Fugue, D (c1720)
Das wohltemperirte Clavier
(The Well-Tempered Keyboard. '48'),
(1722, 1742)
6 English Suites (c1724)
6 French Suites (c1724)
6 Partitas (1731)
Italian Concerto (1735)
French Overture (1735)
Goldberg Variations (1741)
Die Kunst der Fuge (The Art of the Fugue,
c1745)

Organ music
Over 600 chorale preludes.
Concertos, preludes fugues, toccatas,
fantasias, sonatas

understood by scholars to begin around 1600 with such composers as Monteverdi in Italy, Schütz in Germany, Purcell in England and Lully in France. It came to an end around 1750 culminating in the music of Bach, as well as other notable contemporaries – Handel in England, Vivaldi in Italy and Rameau in France. The word 'baroque' comes from the Portuguese *barroco*, or 'misshapen pearl'. It was used later, in the mid 1750s, to describe the art and architecture of the past, which was felt to be over-elaborate in its design. At the same time, musicians adopted the term to express the notion of extravagance and irregularity in music. The 'Classical' period which followed was keen to simplify, refine and regularize this musical language.

Johann Sebastian Bach, the youngest of eight children, was born in 1685 in Eisenach in the central German region of Thuringia. During that period every local court had its own band of musicians and each city its own official music-makers. Bach himself came from an extremely musical family. His father, Johann Ambrosias, was a trumpeter and violinist employed by the ducal court of Eisenach; his uncles and brothers had renowned careers as keyboard players, organists and chamber musicians. Bach's rich musical heritage was further enhanced by his family religion, which was Lutheran. In 1521 Martin Luther, the founder of the Reformation, had fled from Catholic authorities and hidden in Eisenach's castle where he translated the Bible into German. His poetry and hymns would have a profound effect on Bach throughout his life.

Bach's secure family upbringing came to a sudden end in 1694, when he was nine, with the death of his mother, followed a year later by the death of his father. He was taken in by his elder brother Johann Christoph, an organist, who gave him his first formal keyboard lessons. His fine singing voice earned him a scholarship at a school for poor boys at Lüneberg and, aged eighteen, he secured his first employment as organist at the Neue Kirche at Arnstadt. But the church authorities soon found that their brilliant young organist had a fierce musical ambition, and were particularly upset by the elaborate variations he added to Lutheran hymn tunes. But for the gifted young composer, with his intense enthusiasm for new musical ideas and fresh harmonies, playing hymns for a congregation interested only in straightforward musical leadership must have been extremely tedious. Bach became determined to develop his skills as a keyboard virtuoso and, aged twenty, he took a month's leave of absence and walked 200 miles to meet the great Danish organist Dietrich Buxtehude in Lübeck. Buxtehude composed much of his church music for the *Abendmusiken* (evening musical devotions) which were held during the advent season at Lübeck and attracted musicians from all over Germany. They were quasi-dramatic musical spectacles that included dialogues, arias and choruses as well as instrumental pieces and music for organ. The purpose of these musical evenings was to offer the listener something unusual with an – often virtuoso – element of surprise and excitement. Buxtehude's music was no exception. His technique, showmanship and dramatic sense of composition greatly influenced Bach, who stayed away from Arnstadt four times as long as his employers had allowed. They were furious on his return, complaining of his stubbornness as well as other misdemeanours, including inviting a 'strange maiden' into the choir loft. This was probably Bach's cousin, Maria Barbara, whom he married on 17 October 1707.

Bach and Maria Barbara began their married life in Mühlhausen. Here Bach wrote his first cantatas, vocal works consisting of 'recitatives' – narrative passages where the vocal line is similar to the normal patterns of speech – and 'arias', more song-like and lyrical, offering the singer opportunities for emotional expression. The technical fluency, variety of colour and wide expressive range of Bach's early cantatas is impressive. Written in his early twenties, they are stylistically mature and reveal his skill in combining text and music. At Mühlhausen Bach became dissatisfied with the lack of regular church music on Sundays and found it difficult to work with the pastor, whose musical taste was too simple for the ambitious composer. After a year Bach left to become organist and chamber musician at the court of Duke Wilhelm Ernst of Weimar. The duke was devoted to the arts, and his court exposed Bach to a far greater range of international music, particularly when, in 1713, the duke's musical son brought back, from Amsterdam, a selection of scores by a composer who was to have a dramatic influence on Bach – Antonio Vivaldi (1678–1741).

Bach copied and arranged more than ten of Vivaldi's concertos and learned from his Italian contemporary, above all, how to begin a piece with real drama. Bach had a natural feeling for continuity and synthesis, but before studying Vivaldi he was unable to begin a piece in a truly dramatic manner. His later music incorporated strong, dramatic and memorable themes, fusing the Italian Baroque tradition with his own German – and Lutheran – musical heritage. During this period Bach also developed a highly skilled facility in counterpoint (the art of combining any number of melodic lines) and used it as a creative tool to marry different styles and ideas. Bach perfected this method of composing to such a degree that his counterpoint is now regarded as the finest example of its kind in Western music.

At the court in Weimar, he composed organ and chamber pieces, orchestral suites and cantatas. Music at Weimar was required for both

One of Bach's major influences, the Italian composer Antonio Vivaldi

devotional works – at the chapel – and for princely entertainment; Bach ingeniously used the same melodies and popular dance rhythms in his music for both. Whether celebrating the Elector or praising God, he saw himself as 'servant' of either the Christian God or secular Lord. At Weimar Bach became an extremely competent functional artist. He stayed there for nine years, but decided to leave after he was denied the position of Kapellmeister, the musical director responsible for all court music. Insulted by this rebuff and impatient to move on, he insisted on a release from his duties in such an obstinate and abusive manner that the duke had him imprisoned for a month. In 1717, aged thirty-two, he took a post at Cöthen as musical director, where he was concerned chiefly with chamber and orchestral music. He later described his years there as the happiest of his life.

The orchestral cornerstone of Bach's years at Cöthen are his Brandenburg Concertos, commissioned by Christian Ludwig, Margrave of Brandenburg. Their unusual and impressive instrumental groupings and the resulting variety of colours were almost without precedent in orchestral music. In

'I play "The Well-Tempered Clavier" every day of my life... It's like taking a shower and cleansing yourself. It gives you all the feelings of dexterity – you feel like dancing and you are happy to be alive.'

— ANDRAS SCHIFF

the Fifth Concerto he broke further ground by including an extravagant virtuoso cadenza for harpsichord in one of the movements. At Cöthen Bach also promoted the study and composition of keyboard music by writing *Das wohltemperirte Klavier* ('The Well-Tempered Clavier', popularly known as the '48'). This was a collection of 'preludes', short introductory pieces, and 'fugues', music in which different melodic lines, imitating each other, are developed within a set format and structure. Bach composed the collection 'for the profit of the musical youth desirous of learning', but it was also in response to a fundamental change in the tuning of keyboard instruments. Every keyboard presented a series of 'octaves', each of which was made up of eight white notes (CDEFGABC) and five black notes (C sharp or D flat, D sharp or E flat etc). Manufacturers had previously tuned keyboards by intervals of perfect 'fifths' (e.g. C–G) and, as a result, the smaller intervals between the white and black notes (such as the 'semitones' between C and C sharp, or A and B flat) were quite unequal in pitch. Performers and composers therefore had to be content with a limited range of keys – groups of notes corresponding to one 'tonal centre' or individual note. But tuning the instrument by the semitones themselves corrected this inequality, and the new 'well-tempered' tuning made it possible to play adequately in all possible keys. Each key consisted of two variable groups of notes or 'scales', either 'minor' or 'major', depending on the mood of the piece. There were, therefore, 24 possible keys in which now to compose. Bach's completed work of 24 preludes and 24 fugues (48 in all) is a towering achievement in keyboard music, and shows the prelude and fugue form developed to its greatest maturity.

Composers such as Mozart, Beethoven, Chopin and, much later, Béla Bartók, played from the '48' nearly every day of their lives – at the same time learning how to compose by performing Bach on the piano. Later, in the twentieth century, the cellist Pablo Casals called the work 'the old testament of music'. The pianist András Schiff says that '[the preludes and fugues] represent something ... pure to the spirit and the soul', adding that the sensations of movement and dexterity that they provide eliminate the need for technical exercises. There is no line, or voice, which is not interesting in itself, and in all Bach's keyboard works, often consisting of three or four melodic lines played at once, the inner voices, as much as the outer, communicate a unique richness of expression. His music, in the century after his death, became a manual for composers, revealing to them all the possibilities of music through the contrapuntal textures, large-scale tonal structures and, within that structure, new harmonic adventure.

In May 1720 Bach accompanied Prince Leopold of Cöthen to Karlsbad, leaving his wife to look after their four children. In Bach's absence Maria

THE PIANO KEYBOARD

Barbara fell ill and died, possibly as a result of an unsuccessful pregnancy. The news of her death only reached Bach on his return home in July, when she had already been buried. He was now a widower with four young children. The following year, on 3 December 1721, he married Anna Magdalene Wilcke, a fine soprano and the daughter of a court trumpeter. The marriage was romantically and musically fulfilling and would last twenty-nine years, producing thirteen children. Bach's home was a musical workshop. Manuscripts indicate that Anna Magdalena, his students and his children acted as copyists. But there is no mistaking the manuscripts in Bach's own hand, which are remarkably fluent, dense yet crystal clear. The beautiful florid lines of his notation seem almost to reveal his music's emotional and romantic intensity.

In 1723 his work at Cöthen was compromised when the prince was asked for military support by Prussia and had less money available for court entertainment. With a large family and an uncertain future, Bach found alternative employment in the university town of Leipzig. Aged thirty-eight he was appointed Kapellmeister and Kantor (choirleader) of St Thomas's Church, a prestigious post that made him, in effect, the director of music for the entire city. He was to remain in Leipzig for the rest of his life.

During an ordinary working week Bach would have to prepare a cantata for the Sunday service. Such a cantata would set texts of Biblical passages or hymns and more poetic personal texts, musically expressed through chorales, arias, recitatives and short concerted instrumental pieces. It was an exhausting procedure. After picking a text, the first musical thoughts Bach entered on his score were usually the choruses. Then he would add the arias and recitatives before, finally, the concluding chorale. Once the score was finished all the parts had to be copied – first the choral parts (the choir had to be rehearsed first), then the strings, the wind, and finally the basso continuo. Rehearsals began on Friday and on Saturday he would hear the work as a whole for the first time before its performance on Sunday morning. By 1725 Bach had written, rehearsed and performed

The complexity of Bach's instrumental and orchestral music stretched a performer's technical ability to its limits.

two complete cycles of cantatas, and two more by 1729, making a staggering total of 240 substantial compositions in just six years. In this time he had also composed two Magnificats, a Christmas Oratorio, a series of chorale preludes for organ and a 'notebook' of keyboard compositions for Anna Magdalena.

Bach's tenure at Leipzig did not always run smoothly, since he was determined always to fight for his due. He continually argued about both his salary and working conditions, forcing confrontations and controversies with all authorities, appropriate or otherwise. In one argument over his salary he went straight to the Duke of Saxony with his problem, having an apparently over-elevated sense of his own importance.

'The St Matthew Passion expresses something that is permanently there, whether you believe it or not – which is the fact we're here to suffer, and that our profession is to die.'

— JONATHAN MILLER

But despite Bach's dissatisfaction with his daily working life, his creative ambition was unstoppable. In 1727 he gathered together the choirs of the churches as well as musicians from all over Leipzig to perform his extraordinary masterpiece, the *St Matthew Passion* – a narrated drama involving recitative, dialogue, meditation, dramatic incident, arias and chorales. Passions telling the story of the suffering of Christ dated back to medieval times, but this work was of a scale unprecedented in Western religious music. Bach was alone among his contemporaries (and almost unique in the history of music) in his ability to integrate the most dissonant and expressive harmonies into a stable structure and 'consonant' background. The *St Matthew Passion* is a unique example of this style of writing as well as being one of the most emotionally powerful of religious works.

Towards the end of his life Bach began to draw together the strands of his musical output. His Mass in B minor, unperformed in his lifetime, consists of music composed between 1714 and 1749 – an extraordinary thirty-five years. It is both an anthology and a summation of his choral writing, spanning a vast array of styles from Gregorian chant and early Renaissance music to Italian opera. One of the qualities of this work which makes it so appealing to twentieth-century audiences is the integration of dance motifs that appear to drive the whole piece. The Cum Sancto Spiritu is a good example. Bach's ideas here are taken directly from the secular world, the world of theatre music, of ceremonial music, sometimes even of military music, but with a triple-rhythm dance pulse, such as may have been heard at the French court of Louis XIV. It enriches the music with relentless energy but, at the same time, a strong sense of devotional celebration.

By 1748 Bach's health was beginning to fail. His constitution was further undermined by two unsuccessful cataract operations. But, despite the threat of possible blindness, he continued working, almost certainly on his *Die Kunst der Fuge* ('The Art of the Fugue'). Like the Mass in B minor it is a compendium of his musical thoughts and ideas, aimed to exemplify all forms of fugal writing. As with *Das wohltemperirte Clavier* and other works of his mature period, it concentrates on a single aspect of composition within a large unified design. This complex work was unfinished at Bach's death, and appears to end suddenly during the fugue *Contrapunctus 14*. The third section of this fugue is remarkable as it is based on Bach's name – in other words, the fugue's theme is taken from the notes B–A–C–H; in German B stands for B flat, and H for B natural. It was the first time that Bach used his name as a fugue subject and, as a result, this final movement is a particularly moving personal testimony to his art.

Bach died on 28 July 1750, aged sixty-five, leaving over one thousand pieces of music. His monumental legacy is all the more extraordinary considering he was hardly known internationally during his lifetime and his work enjoyed little public recognition until over 80 years after his death. His music is the most difficult music intellectually and technically, but it also has the most powerful emotional effect on its listeners. As the writer Karen Armstrong says, 'Bach seems to be able to articulate feelings, yearnings and huge moments of pathos that enable us to relate to something greater than ourselves.' Yet his music is not for the dilettante. Its difficulty and complexity not only reflects his own extraordinary quest for perfection but also reveals an incredible technical mastery over almost every facet of his musical heritage.

Mozart
and the Enlightenment

OLFGANG AMADEUS MOZART was history's first
great freelance composer. His development of the symphony and concerto
as popular forms was born out of a new social trend in eighteenth-century
Europe – the demand for public concerts by the rising and increasingly
affluent middle classes. The progressive ideas of Joseph II's reign in Vienna,
which encouraged freedom of speech and thought, allowed Mozart to
break free from the chains of patronage and manage his own affairs as an
independent agent. But above all, it is Mozart's mythologized biography,
from *wunderkind* childhood to premature and obscure death, that still
defines our popular conception of a great composer. Only a few decades
after their deaths, the music of Bach and Handel was very much out of
fashion, and the influence of both church and royalty – through patronage

WOLFGANG AMADEUS MOZART – MAJOR WORKS

Operas
Idomeneo (1781)
Die Entführung aus dem Serail (The Abduction from the Seraglio, 1782)
Le nozze di Figaro (The Marriage of Figaro, 1786)
Don Giovanni (1787)
Cosi fan tutte (1790)
Die Zauberflöte (The Magic Flute, 1791)
Le clemenza di Tito (1791)

41 Symphonies including:
No. 31 'Paris', D (1778)
No. 35 'Haffner', D (1782)
No. 36 'Linz', C (1783)
No. 38 'Prague', D (1786)
No. 39 E flat (1788)
No. 40 g (1788)
No. 41 'Jupiter', C (1788)

Concertos
27 piano concertos:
No. 20 d, K. 466 (1785)
No. 21 C, K. 467 (1785)
No. 22 E flat, K. 482 (1785)
No. 23 A, K. 488 (1786)
No. 24 c, K. 491 (1786)
No. 25 C, K. 503 (1786)
No. 26 'Coronation', D, K. 537 (1788)
No. 27 B flat, K. 595 (1791)

5 violin concertos
Sinfonia concertante for violin and viola, K. 364 (1779)
Concertos for bassoon, clarinet, flute and harp, oboe

Other orchestral music
Serenata notturna, K. 239 (1776)
Eine kleine Nachtmusik, K. 525 (1787)

Choral music
18 masses including:
No. 16 'Coronation' (1779)
No. 18 c, (1783, unfinished)
Requiem (1791, unfinished)
Exsultate jubilate (1773)

Chamber music
23 string quartets including:
'Haydn Quartets' – G, K387, d, K. 421 (1783–5).
'Dissonance', C, K. 465 (1785)
'Prussian Quartets' (1789–90)
6 string quintets – C, K. 515 (1787)
clarinet quintet

Piano music
17 sonatas, rondos, variations, fantasias, and works for two pianos

– was steadily diminishing. Mozart's music epitomizes what musicians refer to as the 'Classical' style – a refined unity of expression and form which represented, at the time, a complete break from what was regarded as the bombastic ugliness of the Baroque.

Wolfgang Amadeus Mozart was born in Salzburg on 27 January 1756. His father, Leopold Mozart, was assistant director of the archbishop's chapel. Leopold was a composer, the author of a respected treatise on violin playing, and an excellent teacher. Mozart could play the harpsichord by the time he was four, compose when he was five and started touring Europe to become music's most famous child prodigy when he was six. He went on to compose his first symphony when he was eight, his first oratorio at eleven and his first opera aged twelve. A prodigy, however, can only develop within a conducive social environment. A child composer with Mozart's talent might not have thrived a hundred years earlier. Not only was he fortunate to have had a brilliant teacher in his father, but he was brought into contact with almost every kind of music during his travels in western Europe. He imitated these different styles in his own works but, at the same time, improved on his models. Mozart's early compositions therefore mirrored the music of the period and transformed it through his own genius.

The first major influence on Mozart was the composer J. C. Bach, the youngest son of Johann Sebastian. They met when Mozart was eight and giving concerts in London. Bach enjoyed huge success in this major city which had a thriving concert life. Wealthy audiences demanded a new style of music that was appealing and dramatic, but also structured in an easily recognizable and satisfying manner. Bach had mastered this in his symphonies, which were often composed in three movements, in the Italian tradition – fast-slow-fast. The structure of each movement was based on what was subsequently termed 'sonata form' – simply put, two musical ideas (usually contrasting) are stated, and then developed in different, but related keys, before being restated in the original 'home' key, bringing the movement to a close. There are well-defined contrasts in Bach's symphonies, and his slow movements are warm, graceful and expressive. He combined the best features of the German and Italian traditions, and it is not surprising that the young Mozart was attracted to this music and soon adapted and developed its style for his own symphonic music. But it was not until Mozart was in his early teenage years that he began fully to develop as a composer, and it was opera that led him towards maturity as a musician.

Leopold Mozart appears to have encouraged his son to write opera because he believed it would guarantee fame for the young composer. Italian opera was dominant at the time, both *opera seria* (grand opera on a heroic or tragic subject) and *opera buffa* (comic opera). Mozart made his first attempts at the form during tours of Italy in the early 1770s. His first Italian opera, an *opera seria*, *Mitridate, rè di Ponto*, was produced in Milan

The phenomenon of
the miniature Mozart
was soon introduced to
every court in Europe.
The world's most
famous child prodigy
had been born.

and its success enabled Mozart's family to move from their modest flat in Salzburg to a house in a more elegant location. Mozart's opera experience began to influence his instrumental writing. In one of his first early masterpieces, the A major Violin Concerto (1775), the soloist enters with material quite different to the preceding orchestral passage; this separate, contrasting statement for the concerto's soloist finds a clear parallel in Mozart's operatic writing for orchestra and vocal soloists of the same period. Possibly the best of Mozart's *opera seria* is his later *Idomeneo* (1781), the music of which, despite a clumsy libretto, is both dramatic and pictorial. Its conspicuous use of chorus and its creation of spectacular scenes was modelled on Mozart's

'I think Mozart is the God of music. I loved him when I was a child and I still enjoy Mozart's music as I enjoy no other. There is something special about this man which is irresistible.'

———————— SIR COLIN DAVIS

contemporary Christoph Gluck (1714–87). Gluck's talent for creating dramatic moments by using simple techniques in such operas as *Orfeo ed Euridice* (1762) had made him famous throughout Europe.

Mozart was now highly successful as a composer, but unable to find suitable employment in Salzburg. In 1778 he left for Paris, accompanied by his mother, to seek a prestigious post in the French capital. Mozart knew that he would only achieve success there if his music was popular with the Parisian audiences. His showy, exuberant 'Paris' Symphony (1778) was calculated to please. The work was very well received, but overall the trip was not a success. Although Mozart's stature as a composer had steadily increased (he had by then written such works as the Piano Concerto in E flat, K. 271, and the Symphonie Concertante for violin and viola), he failed to find permanent employment in Paris. To add to this misfortune, his mother fell ill during their stay in Paris and died. Remarkably, Mozart wrote to his father of the 'Paris' Symphony's success, making no mention of his mother, who was, at the same moment, lying dead in the next room. We know that Mozart was desperately worried about breaking this tragic news to his father. But perhaps his letter also tells us something about Mozart's detached view of the world and approach to his art – where the mundane occurrences of daily life appeared to be but shadowy parallels to the paramount concerns of his creativity. This has been the popular view of Mozart over the centuries, but some eminent scholars now disagree. For example, the pianist and musicologist Robert Levin recognizes in Mozart's A minor Piano Sonata, K. 310 an overwhelming emotion that had not been heard before in Mozart's music, and he connects this with Mozart's traumatic experience of losing his mother. Levin says that there is 'something absolutely psychotic' about the music, and that the last movement can only be understood as a 'paroxysm of a man who's over the edge'.

By 1779 Mozart had been forced to return home. Frustrated at being a mere Konzertmeister in the provincial Salzburg court he set his sights on Vienna. At that time Vienna was experiencing one of the most exciting decades of its history. In 1780 the pro-Enlightenment Emperor Joseph II took the Habsburg throne, cutting aristocratic rights, raising the status of the middle class and declaring freedom of speech. These acts became law in June 1781, just as Mozart decided to move to Vienna. Ever aware of his prodigious talent, Mozart had always wished to be treated as an equal by the ruling aristocracy. In Vienna his ambitions would be realized.

One of Joseph II's first musical reforms was to crush the domination of Italian opera in his theatres and promote a new nationalistic 'German' opera. Mozart now began work on his first 'German' opera, *Die Entführung aus der Serail* ('The Abduction from the Seraglio'). This took the form of a *singspiel*, a German-language opera which used songs and spoken dialogue rather than continuous music. It was an immediate success. Mozart found the new Vienna both sympathetic and stimulating, making friends with a number of cultural and intellectual figures. He also became committed to freemasonry. The group of masons with which he associated was a kind of literary or scientific academy, committed to promoting Enlightenment ideas in science, politics and literature. With no patron or employer, Mozart had become effectively the first freelance composer in Vienna's thriving modern economy. As well as teaching his many pupils, he was also his own manager, organizing and promoting concerts, running subscription lists, and chasing publishers to get his works into print.

Mozart promoted himself as both pianist and composer, and the single musical form which enabled him to show off all his talents at once was the piano concerto. Although he had written many concertos before he arrived in Vienna, the twelve piano concertos he composed between 1784 and 1786 developed the concerto into the form we recognize it as today. The Baroque concerto had consisted of solo passages which alternated with repeated orchestral sections (ritornellos) stating the main musical material. Mozart turned the concerto into a three-movement structure of symphonic dimensions. The Viennese public recognized and admired his genius as both composer and pianist and flocked to his concerts, but over and above his compositions, and his playing of them, it was Mozart's improvisations, often several in a single concerto, that dazzled his audiences.

In 1782 Mozart married the singer Constanze Weber, whose elder sister he had admired some years earlier. Leopold Mozart did not approve of the match, but his son insisted on marrying for love. Sadly, he met his father on only a few occasions after his marriage and only once did Mozart return to Salzburg.

In Vienna, the Imperial Librarian, Baron Gottfried von Swieten, was a key figure in Joseph II's reforming government, and an ardent admirer of Baroque music. He fired a passionate enthusiasm in Mozart for Bach and Handel. Mozart before then had viewed counterpoint as little more than a superficial way of merging one musical idea with another. After studying the music of the Baroque masters, however, he developed a new technical mastery in writing fugue, which was first revealed in the finale of the G major string quartet. But of all the composers who influenced Mozart in Vienna, the greatest was Joseph Haydn (1732–1809). He wrote over 100

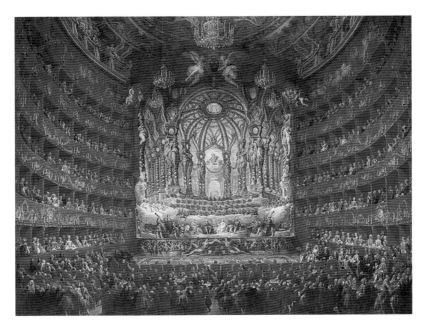

If Mozart wished to be a success in Europe he would have to excel in one genre above all others – opera.

symphonies and is now regarded as the first great exponent of the form. His music is characterized by humour, honest craftsmanship, intellectual sophistication, but also maintains a spiritual contact with his audience. Haydn's string quartets represent a high point in his artistic oeuvre, and Mozart wrote six of his own which he dedicated to Haydn. When Mozart played them to him, with Leopold present, Haydn turned to Leopold, saying, 'I swear to you before God and as an honest man that your son is the greatest composer that I know either personally or by reputation.'

The early 1780s were the greatest years of Mozart's musical career. He was wealthy enough to move into a spacious apartment in the centre of Vienna. It was there that Mozart wrote many masterpieces, including eleven piano concertos, the Haydn string quartets and his opera *Le nozze di Figaro* ('The Marriage of Figaro'). Although Mozart had earlier been committed to German opera, fashion changed once again to favour the Italians. Mozart met the librettist Lorenzo da Ponte, and suggested they turn Beaumarchais' scandalous political play *Le Mariage de Figaro* into an opera. *Le nozze di Figaro* was well received in Vienna but in the neighbouring city of Prague it created a sensation. The opera's story concerns a complex web of relationships between masters and servants in a nobleman's household. There are many eighteenth-century operas about noblemen attempting to seduce country girls, but, in each case, their attempts are frustrated, and virtue triumphs. In Mozart's opera the characters are not the conventional caricatures of the time but recognizable human beings. Mozart's music brings them to life, communicating to the listener their social backgrounds and the sexual tensions that provide the opera's driving force. Unlike other Italian opera, Mozart's melodic lines, suggestive harmony and rich orchestration colour the emotional content of the words of each of his characters.

'Mozart's characters are fragile, passionate and profound. I think that his music is unique. It touches both the heart and mind of any thinking person.'
— CECILIA BARTOLI

Prague, more musically sophisticated than Vienna, appreciated Mozart's richer style. In acknowledgement, Mozart wrote the 'Prague' Symphony and the opera *Don Giovanni* – Da Ponte was once again the collaborator. *Don Giovanni*, despite being a comic opera, is an extraordinarily dark and dramatic work. Its hero is one of the most disturbing and enigmatic characters in all opera. He represents in some sense the overthrowing of traditional practices and morality, which could be associated with 'enlightened' ideas, but he also represents dark irrationality. The opera, importantly, was written in 1787 when opinion over Joseph's reforms was changing after much disillusionment and a desire to return to older values. *Don Giovanni's* music is not only full of drama but, unlike any of Bach or Handel's dramatic music, it possesses a real sense of terror. At its first performance, when Don Giovanni took the hand of the Commendatore and was dragged down to Hell, the audience had never before witnessed anything so frightening in the theatre.

In 1787 Leopold died, and in the same year Mozart's fortunes began to change. Vienna's economy was fragile and Mozart was no longer the musician of the moment. His commissions began to dwindle and his subscribers disappeared. But despite rising debt, and his life appearing to crumble around him, Mozart wrote some of his greatest music. The string quartets of the period are among the best in the repertoire, and his last three, highly popular symphonies were written remarkably quickly during the summer of 1788. The last two are in G minor and C, the same keys as two of his string quintets. The G minor symphony is highly original in the grace and restrained passion of its opening theme, the first three notes of which are used in different combinations to drive the entire movement. The finest example of Mozart's counterpoint can be found in the C major symphony (the 'Jupiter'). Its last movement is a sonata-form structure interwoven with fugal sections, and towards the end of the movement Mozart demonstrates an extraordinary command over his material, bringing together every single musical element in a passage of unique complexity and excitement.

By 1791 Mozart's fortunes were improving. He was the proud father of two sons and still happily married with, once again, a flourishing career. His latest opera, *Die Zauberflöte* ('The Magic Flute'), which includes masonic symbolism, was hugely successful. New commissions kept him busy, in particular one from a Count Walsegg-Stuppach who wanted Mozart to compose a Requiem in memory of his wife. Mozart began the Requiem, but it was never finished. On 18 November he became seriously ill and died of kidney failure as a result of an influenza epidemic that was sweeping Vienna. His body was taken to St Mark's cemetery on the city's outskirts and his modest third-class burial was entirely in accordance with the Emperor Joseph II's reformed rules on burial practice.

For centuries Mozart has represented the idea of the sublime in music. Certainly, perfection of form and musical structure was something to which he aspired all his life. But he found the process of composing far more difficult than we have been led to believe. The vast number of musical sketches for works which never materialized is testimony to the effort and anguish he poured into his compositions. His music is so completely satisfying, however, that his compositions seem to be miraculously effortless. It is, perhaps, for this reason that Mozart, rather than Haydn, became the hero of the Romantic generation which followed.

Beethoven
and early Romanticism

THE CREATIVE GENIUS and the remarkably expressive power of Ludwig van Beethoven's compositions have established him as one of the most admired composers in musical history. It is possible to argue that everything he wrote was intended for posterity, and the idea of the composer becoming, in effect, immortal through the power of his art was a new departure in music. The notion of the artist as 'hero' is strikingly convincing in Beethoven's case since he composed most of his works while going through the immensely traumatic experience of becoming deaf. His belief in the strength of the human spirit and his musical representation of the power of Nature sowed the seeds for Romanticism in music. Indeed, his music can be seen as a bridge between the Classical and Romantic eras. It embodied a new dynamism and power

LUDWIG VAN BEETHOVEN – MAJOR WORKS

Symphonies
No. 1, C (1800)
No. 2, D (1802)
No. 3, 'Eroica', E flat (1803)
No. 4, B flat (1806)
No. 5, c (1808)
No. 6, 'Pastoral', F (1808)
No. 7, A (1812)
No. 8, F (1812)
No. 9, 'Choral', d (1824)

Concertos
5 piano concertos
Violin Concerto, D (1806)
Triple Concerto for piano, violin
and cello, C (1804)

Overtures and incidental music
Coriolan (1807).
Leonore Overtures
nos. 1, 2 and 3 (1805–6)
Egmont (1810)

Opera
Fidelio (1805, revised 1806, 1814)

Choral music
Mass in D (Missa solemnis, 1819-23)

Piano music
32 sonatas:
No. 8 'Pathétique', c, op. 13 (1799)

No. 14 'Moonlight', c sharp,
op. 27 no. 2 (1801)
No. 21 'Waldstein', C, op. 53 (1804)
No. 23 'Appassionata', f, (1805)
No. 26 'Les adieux', E flat,
op. 81a (1799)
No. 29 'Hammerklavier', B flat,
op. 106 (1818)

String quartets
Opus 18, nos. 1–6 (1798–1800)
Opus 59, nos. 1–3 'Razumovsky
Quartets' (1806)
Op. 127 (1824)
Op. 132 (1825)
Op. 130 (1826)
Op. 133, 'Grosse Fuge' (1826)
Op. 131 (1826)
Op. 135 (1826)

Other chamber music
Piano trios: Opus 97, 'Archduke' (1811)'
String quintets
Piano quintet
Sonatas for piano and violin
Octet for wind instruments (1793)

Songs
An die ferne Geliebte
(To the Distant Beloved), song cycle
for tenor and piano (1816)

which symbolized the changing role of the composer in society. He was no longer its lowly servant but, instead, a visionary.

Beethoven was born in Bonn and baptized on 17 December 1770. His father was a court singer in Bonn; his grandfather had been Kapellmeister at the same court. Ludwig's father recognized his son's special musical talent and planned to use it to his financial advantage, emulating Mozart's father who had taken the young Wolfgang all over Europe. Beethoven was forced to practise piano, violin and organ.

When he was only nine he performed all the preludes and fugues of J. S. Bach's *Das wohltemperirte Clavier* ('The Well-Tempered Clavier') in public – shortly after his teacher, Christian Neefe, obtained a manuscript copy of the then little known work. Beethoven soon became assistant organist to the Elector of Bonn and his teacher claimed that he would, indeed, become a second Mozart. Whenever a new opera by Mozart was performed in Vienna, the score would eventually reach Bonn and be devoured by the young Beethoven. In 1787, aged sixteen, he managed to go to Vienna and meet the great composer. Mozart heaped praises on him, predicting a great future. But tragically, Beethoven's mother died during his visit and he had to leave the city immediately. When he returned to Vienna five years later, Mozart had died.

Following his mother's death, Beethoven's father, an alcoholic, was unfit to look after his family, so Ludwig took on the responsibility. He became a viola player in the local chapel orchestra, excelled as a pianist and quickly developed as a composer. When Austria's Emperor Joseph II died, Beethoven was asked by the Elector of Bonn to compose a commemorative cantata. This powerful early work has an intensity of style – particularly in its use of dramatic motifs and its distinctive range of dynamics – that is uniquely Beethovenian. The composer had, at the age of only 19, found his voice.

In August 1792 Louis XVI of France was arrested during the French Revolution. In October the Elector fled Bonn as French troops approached the city. Beethoven followed a week later to study with Joseph Haydn in Vienna. He would never return to his birthplace. Vienna was then an exciting and vibrant city, full of energy and frivolity – but a frivolity tinged with fear and despair. Austria was terrified of the consequences of the Revolution and the possibility of a French invasion. Censorship was tightened, and the secret police were given extra powers to seek out spies and intruders. Instrumental music, however, was the most abstract and least censorable of the arts, and composers continued to flourish.

Beethoven learned little from Haydn's teaching but a great deal from his music. His own compositions developed within Mozart and Haydn's Classical framework, but they had a new, almost aggressive urgency and a rougher, more boisterous edge. Many listeners found his music

unattractive, complex and even bizarre. The opening movement of Beethoven's first published piano sonata, in F minor, shows at once the urgency of his musical voice in its impetuous opening. Beethoven's piano-playing was both brilliant and highly emotional. Viennese audiences, ill at ease with the unusual intensity of Beethoven's music, also resented its intellectual demands. Beethoven refused to have his music treated as mere background entertainment and insisted his audience try to appreciate and understand its melodic invention and creative structure.

The Austrian composer Joseph Haydn, who gave lessons to Beethoven, and whose music was a great influence.

Beethoven's style of piano playing was also criticized – the ferocious energy of his performances would often result in broken strings.

The outstanding characteristic of Beethoven's music, compared with his predecessors Mozart and Haydn, was its demonic energy. Because of its controversial nature his music needed a careful introduction; Beethoven also required someone to find venues for performances, enlist musicians and engage publishers. For all of this he acquired the help of wealthy patrons. One such patron was Prince Lichnowsky, who not only arranged concerts for the composer but also staged improvisation contests between Beethoven and other Viennese virtuosos. It was with Lichnowsky that he embarked on his first concert tour, in 1796, to Prague, Dresden and Berlin.

Beethoven had always made rough drafts of his works, often on various scraps of paper. With his Op. 18 set of string quartets (1798–90), he began to organize his musical ideas more systematically. He started to use sketchbooks, which grew to contain hundreds of musical fragments. He would wander in the countryside and scribble down musical ideas as they came to him. It was through this sketching process that he was able later to develop a musical language that was more complex than anything he had written before.

Beethoven's first two symphonies date from around 1800, but they do not share the passionate style of his other early works, notably the 'Pathétique' piano sonata. Although his attempts at orchestral writing are highly accomplished at this stage, it is clear that his ability to express the very depths of emotion was still to emerge in this genre. It was during this time that Beethoven went into a deep depression. Around 1796 he had began to have problems with his hearing. 'My ears continue to buzz and hum day and night,' he wrote. 'I can hear sounds, it's true, but cannot make out the words.' By 1798, while becoming successful as a composer, he became acutely aware that he was losing his hearing. Doctors urged him not to worry, but the condition worsened. In 1802, after months of suicidal despair, he wrote what has become known as the Heiligenstadt Testament. It is a moving account: Beethoven accepts that he is losing his hearing, but vows to continue to struggle for the sake of his art until, as he said, 'I'd produced all that I felt was in me.'

The first work Beethoven composed after writing the testament was, tellingly, his oratorio *Christ on the Mount of Olives* – the composer must surely have identified with the suffering, loneliness and isolation of Christ on the eve of his crucifixion. The other work he wrote immediately after the Heiligenstadt Testament was his third symphony, the 'Eroica' (1803), the cornerstone of Beethoven's 'heroic' period. The most striking element of this symphony is its length – roughly twice that of any symphony by Mozart or Haydn. The melodies used in this symphony are more like short motifs, developed and combined within a huge edifice. The symphony is the story

> *'The melodies [in the 'Eroica'] are so simple, the materials are so simple – every brick is simple, but the building is incredible.'*
> —— NIKOLAUS HARNONCOURT

of a hero, and it was originally dedicated to the great republican Napoleon Bonaparte. But when Napoleon crowned himself Emperor, Beethoven flew into a rage, erasing the name Bonaparte so violently from the manuscript that there is a hole in the original score. He uses a higher level of dissonance in the 'Eroica' than in any previous symphony, possibly as a frustrating representation of the unbearable 'noises' in his ears.

Beethoven was now enjoying recognition as a composer but his personal life was not as successful. He gave piano lessons to women from wealthy families, and fell in love with many of these aristocratic pupils. To one of them, Countess Giulietta Guicciardi, he dedicated his famous Piano Sonata in C sharp minor, the 'Moonlight', in 1801. Giulietta had a cousin, Josephine von Brunsvik, whose relationship with Beethoven became closer when she was widowed in 1804. Josephine's feelings for Beethoven are not known, but for him it was an important relationship.

There are thirteen love letters written by Beethoven to Josephine before 1808, and in one of them he wrote, 'You are my return to life from my crisis over my deafness', and followed this by composing a huge volume of music including the first attempt at his only opera *Fidelio* (1805), the 'Razumovsky' string quartets (1806), the Violin Concerto in D (1806) and his Fifth and Sixth Symphonies. Frustratingly, little is known of how the affair progressed or ended.

In sympathy with his personal life, Beethoven's domestic situation, as he became more deaf, was chaotic and unsettled. He never stayed for long in one place and lived at thirty or forty different addresses in Vienna. Possessions often disappeared or were damaged. Beethoven spent ten years, on and off, at a residence known as the Pasqualati House. Contemporary writers described his home there as the 'dirtiest, most disorderly place imaginable'.

One of the legacies of the revolutionary period was the idea of making gestures or statements for posterity. Parisian orators, such as Robespierre, felt they were speaking not just to their assembled audiences but to the world at large, both then and in the future. Their speeches were crafted through the development of a striking idea or theme, which they would return to again and again. Beethoven, similarly, makes forceful and gripping musical statements, develops them, then returns to them relentlessly. The famous Fifth Symphony (1808), with its persistent opening four-note motif, is a good example. The work has been described by Nikolaus Harnoncourt not as music but as 'political agitation', a 'manifestation of ideas' in which Beethoven appears to be deploring dictatorship. Napoleon briefly occupied Vienna in 1805, and the Fifth Symphony became a symbol for the people's triumph over oppression. At the time of its first public performance, in December 1808, Napoleon was again threatening to invade Vienna, and Beethoven began another colossal work with military themes – the 'Emperor' Piano Concerto. But, for the first time, he did not play the solo part at its première; he had become too deaf. Beethoven would never complete another piano concerto. However, he insisted on continuing to conduct his own compositions, and presented a bizarre, comical yet poignant sight.

As his deafness deteriorated Beethoven's personal life became more desperate. Scholars remain fascinated by a passionate love-letter written by Beethoven on 5 July 1812. Intriguingly, he does not name the woman who inspired this extraordinary passion, referring to her only as his 'immortal beloved'. Some musicologists believe her to be Josephine von Brunsvik, whose earlier affair with Beethoven is presumed to have faded, but another contender is Antonie Brentano, as her movements roughly correspond with those alluded to in the letter. Previous letters which survive from Beethoven to his old love, Josephine, however, match the letter of 1812 in passion, style and vocabulary. Interestingly, both women had children eight or nine months after the letter was written; one of these children might, therefore, have been Beethoven's child. Antonie had a boy, who suffered from epilepsy, Josephine a girl, who turned out to be extremely musical and who later became a piano teacher. In the last decade of Beethoven's life, in one of his 'conversation books' (notebooks supplied to his friends and colleagues so that they could communicate with him), there is an entry: 'if you talk about the child so much, people will know that it's yours.' No gender is mentioned, but this certainly suggests that Beethoven believed he had fathered a child.

Married love is the subtitle of the opera *Fidelio*, in which a woman disguises herself as a man to rescue her husband from prison. The opera director Peter Hall explains that Beethoven was obsessed with the theme of *Fidelio* (he wrote and re-wrote the opera over twelve years) because he empathized with its hero, a man living in a dark prison – like a deaf man – waiting to be rescued from that loneliness by an adoring woman. '[Beethoven] writes about love as well as anybody,' says Peter Hall. 'It's resolved love ... So I think the man–woman relationship and the power and potency of love is even more important than the other great theme of *Fidelio*, which is freedom – freedom of speech, freedom of behaviour, and horror of a totalitarian or fascist rule.'

Fidelio was finally performed to great acclaim in 1814. Beethoven, aged forty-three, had reached the peak of his fame, but his personal life once again became troubled. His brother died and Beethoven found himself joint guardian of his nephew, Karl, together with the child's mother. It

Beethoven dedicated the 'Eroica' symphony to Napoleon Bonaparte, but erased his name from the manuscript when Bonaparte crowned himself Emperor.

was a time of turmoil for Beethoven, who was very conscious that his nephew was the only Beethoven of the next generation. In 1815 a five-year custody battle began, and Beethoven used every means to take the boy from his mother.

During this time, as Beethoven's deafness became more profound he composed steadily less. But this also seems to have been a kind of gestation period for him before he emerged with a new style. The resulting 'Hammerklavier' Piano Sonata, Op. 106 (1818) is widely accepted as one of Beethoven's greatest works, written when the composer could no longer hear himself play at the piano. Vladimir Ashkenazy has suggested that it marks Beethoven's transition from the material to a more spiritual world. It has perhaps the most openly tragic slow movement that Beethoven wrote. In the last nine years of his life, he was completely deaf, and relied totally on the conversation books as a bridge to the outside world. He became more reclusive and even eccentric, paying little if any attention to his external appearance. He was even arrested as a tramp around 1820.

But, despite his personal trauma, Beethoven continued to compose and asked if London's Philharmonic Society were interested in commissioning a 'grand' symphony. The result was the monumental Ninth Symphony, the 'Choral' (1824). The sketches of its first movement date from 1816, but the idea of setting the text of Schiller's *Ode to Joy* to music (in the huge set of variations that is the finale) comes from as far back as his time in Bonn. The symphony celebrates brotherhood and humanity, and includes some of Beethoven's most lyrical yet intricate music. It was a huge success at its première although, sadly, Beethoven, who had been conducting next to the 'real' conductor, had to be turned around in order to see the tumultuous applause.

'The Adagio [of the 'Hammerklavier'] is beyond description. Some people say it's a final acceptance of something – maybe. But that's only a part of it. It is in a different world.'

——————— VLADIMIR ASHKENAZY

The last of Beethoven's published compositions, the late string quartets, Opp. 130, 131, 133 and 135, were commissioned by the Russian Prince Golitsïn. These quartets are often regarded as Beethoven's greatest body of work, but to many of his contemporaries this strange, inaccessible music was definite proof that the composer had lost his sanity. In these compositions Beethoven challenged the form, style and expression of the string quartet. They are transcendent works, which possess a deeply personal, emotional and spiritual intensity, unique in all music.

Beethoven finally won the long battle of custody for his nephew, but by 1826, Karl, aged nineteen, was desperate to break the bond with his uncle. Beethoven had become obsessed with the fear that Karl would contract the then common and fatal disease of syphilis (the composer Franz Schubert was shortly to die from it), and he tried to interfere in Karl's personal relationships. In a fit of desperation, Karl attempted but failed to commit suicide, afterwards claiming that Beethoven had driven him to it. The tragedy deeply depressed Beethoven during the last months of his life. He was also increasingly unwell, and died, from kidney failure, in Vienna on 26 March 1827, aged fifty-six. His funeral cortège included 200 carriages and there were crowds of over 20,000. In his final will he left everything to Karl.

Beethoven is, arguably, the most enduring of composers. His music stretches the bounds of expressivity to its limits. His depiction of Nature in his music, as well as his musical expression of nostalgia and reminiscence, laid the foundations for the early Romantic movement. His Ninth Symphony, in particular, became one of the most influential works of the entire nineteenth century. Its innovative harmony and structure, including the unprecedented use of a chorus and soloists in the last movement, had a profound effect on future composers, most notably Mahler and Wagner. Wagner indeed idolized Beethoven, and he performed the Ninth Symphony almost every year of his working life, most memorably at the laying of the foundation stone for his own theatre at Bayreuth. But above all, Wagner was able to use Beethoven's example to feed his own ambitions and create an art form that would propel music into the twentieth century.

Wagner
and the
Music Drama

BEETHOVEN had sown the seeds for the Romantic movement in music, but it was Schubert, Schumann, Berlioz, Weber, Mendelssohn, Chopin and Liszt who more fully expressed and developed the mood and ideas of Romanticism in the nineteenth century. The Classical world had been based on form and order, but now emotional expression, instinct and imagination were of paramount importance. The music and ideals of Richard Wagner encapsulate and represent the culmination of so many Romantic characteristics that he can, perhaps, be regarded as the consummate Romantic artist. With his Italian contemporary, Giuseppe Verdi (whose works were completely different in style and philosophy), he dominated opera in the late Romantic era.

Wagner was another revolutionary. He believed that a stage production

RICHARD WAGNER – MAJOR WORKS

Operas
Rienzi (1842)
Der fliegende Holländer (The Flying Dutchman, 1843)
Tannhäuser (1845, revised 1861)
Lohengrin (1850)

Music Dramas
Tristan und Isolde (1865)
Die Meistersinger von Nürnburg (The Mastersingers of Nuremberg, 1876)
Der Ring des Nibelungen
(The Ring of the Nibelung, 1876)

Das Rheingold (The Rhinegold, 1869)
Die Walküre (The Valkyrie, 1870)
Siegfried (1876)
Götterdämmerung
(Twilight of the Gods, 1876)
Parsifal (1882)

Orchestral music
Siegfried Idyll (1870)

Songs
Wesendonck Lieder (1857–8)

should encapsulate every art form – poetry, literature, dance, design, visual spectacle as well as music – and his successful realization of this ambitious aim had a lasting effect on many twentieth-century art forms. His vast opera cycle, *Der Ring des Nibelungen* ('The Ring of the Nibelung'), a musical experience of astounding scale and complexity, is one of the finest achievements of the human mind. But a shadow rests over Wagner's life and reputation. He was notoriously anti-Semitic, and his views, laid out in his diatribe *Das Judenthum in der Musik* ('Judaism in Music') (1850), were later taken up by the Nazi movement in support of its own racist ideology.

Richard Wagner was born in Leipzig on 22 May 1813, the ninth child of Johanna and Carl Friedrich Wagner, a police official. Soon after he was baptized, his father died, and his mother took the family to live with an actor and painter Ludwig Geyer. It is not known if Johanna was having an affair with Geyer, or if Geyer might have been Wagner's real father, but Wagner signed himself Richard Geyer at school and, strangely, only reverted to the name of Wagner at the age of fifteen.

Theodore Weinlich, one of Wagner's earliest teachers, gave him a good grounding in symphonic writing, and Beethoven was one of Wagner's earliest influences. Wagner briefly attended Leipzig University before working as a chorus master in provincial opera houses. He composed his first operas in the early 1830s, while still a teenager. *Die Feen* ('The Fairies') was influenced by Weber, whose *Der Freischütz* was the most popular

German opera of the day; another, *Das Liebesverbot* ('The Ban on Love'), was written in the style of light Italian opera, and performed in Magdeburg in 1836.

When Wagner was twenty-one, he fell in love with, and married, an actress, Minna Planer. It was not a good match – Wagner was intellectually curious and ambitious, Minna socially accomplished, physically attractive, but hardly Wagner's intellectual equal. Money was scarce for the couple, and Wagner began a lifelong habit of borrowing and subsequently getting himself into debt.

He secured his first important post as a conductor at the German opera house in Riga. This theatre was particularly dark, its stalls raked upwards like an Greek amphitheatre, and the orchestra was in a 'sunken' pit, concealed below the stage. Wagner would remember these features later when he built his own ideal theatre at Bayreuth. At Riga he composed the first two acts of *Rienzi*, a 'grand opera' in the French style of the day; it included scenic spectacle as well as dance and large crowd scenes. He also began sketches for his next opera, *Der fliegende Holländer* ('The Flying Dutchman'). But his debts were mounting, and in order to avoid imprisonment, he fled from his creditors. He escaped to the Baltic coast and boarded a ship for Paris. He and Minna arrived there in 1839. They would stay for three years.

Paris was then Europe's most glamorous city, and the centre of the opera world. The Jewish composer Giacomo Meyerbeer, the most successful opera composer in Paris, offered Wagner help. But Wagner failed to secure a single performance of any of his operas. He perceived Parisian musical life to be dominated by a Jewish clique, which he found alien and soon began to despise. He used his outsider status as an excuse for his own failure. To make ends meet, he was obliged to make piano transcriptions of operas by Jacques Halévy, another Jewish composer.

In *Rienzi*, first performed in 1842 at the Dresden Opera House, Wagner tried to surpass Meyerbeer and Halévy in the style of grand opera. *Der fliegende Holländer*, Wagner's first masterpiece, is utterly different in character. Its story reflects one of the fashions of the time – an interest in the supernatural: a sailor is doomed to travel the seas forever until being redeemed by the love of a faithful woman. Wagner's new level of dramatic and psychological observation in this opera (particularly regarding one of the principle characters, Senta) provides a foretaste of his mature music dramas. Its themes of love, death and redemption likewise recur in all his later works.

Rienzi is not one of Wagner's finest operas, but its première in Dresden was the most successful of his whole career. It made him famous in Europe and earned him, aged twenty-nine, the post of Royal

> *'Part of Wagner's fascination is that there are so many people who still feel so incredibly negative and disgusted by him as a musician and as a personality – and that keeps the music alive.'*
>
> —————— DANIEL BARENBOIM

Kapellmeister to the King of Saxony. Wagner now became interested in philosophy and soon acquired a large library at Dresden. He immersed himself in the writings of Hegel, who believed that music had come to an impasse with Beethoven. This gave Wagner the impetus to develop a style of music that would be new in both concept and form.

In his next operas, *Tannhäuser* (1845) and *Lohengrin* (1850), he set out to change the concept of German opera, basing his stories on Teutonic myth and legend. He also pushed the limits of his sound-world to new extremes. His orchestration had all the brilliance of the music of the time, but, as the composer Robin Holloway says, '[Wagner] fills out the gaps. He blocks and ranks his orchestra in choirs so the range of colour is much greater, but also the range of sonority and blend.' *Tannhäuser* is grand opera, but its libretto (which Wagner wrote himself, as he did for all his operas) is in the German Romantic style. It is the story of a knight whose faithful lover buys his redemption with her death after he succumbs to the pleasures of the Venusberg, a mythical world where love reigns free.

Lohengrin tells the tale of a Knight of the Holy Grail who appears miraculously to save a condemned woman, and marries her on condition that she does not ask his name. The sections of this opera are less defined, as Wagner moves towards the musical and textural continuity of his later operas. The orchestration is fuller and also more subtle, with effects such as the multi-layered high string passage at the beginning of the opera's prelude – a quite striking and original style of writing for the time. The Wagner scholar John Deathridge says that with this opera Wagner 'had reached a kind of stretching of music ... the entire opera has been conceived in a very cohesive way to exploit this power of music to draw you in, and to give you the feeling that it's giving you something that you lack in your real life.'

Wagner also based his operatic ideas on Greek tragedy, arguing that it worked well as drama because its mythical subjects were not constrained by history. He recognized that myth enshrined timeless truths, and believed that by incorporating these universal ideas in his music he could change the world in which he lived. But he felt there needed to be social and political change (brought about by revolution) before such artistic and cultural change was possible. The Dresden Revolution of 1848 was therefore timely. It was an attempt to unify Germany from several small nation-states, and Wagner, an ardent nationalist, participated enthusiastically in the uprising. He also believed that this would be the revolution to bring him closer to achieving his radical artistic goals. But the uprising was suppressed, and Wagner fled to avoid prison and possible execution. With the help of the composer Franz Liszt, he found refuge and a home in Zurich.

Wagner, now fired with political fervour, produced a number of theoretical essays. In one, *Das Kunstwerk der Zukunft* ('The Artwork of the Future'), he laid down his criteria for an idealistic art form, which he called the *Gesamtkunstwerk*, or 'total art-form'. This included music, poetry, dance and visual spectacle. Wagner believed that his new performance concept – which he named music drama – would raise art about the level of mere entertainment. He continued to explore these themes in his controversial booklet, *Das Judenthum in der Musik*, in which he held Jews responsible for everything derivative and mediocre in German art.

In Zurich Wagner also began his massive cycle *The Ring of the Nibelung*. It consists of four operas, *Das Rheingold* ('The Rheingold'), *Die Walküre* ('The Valkyrie'), *Siegfried* and *Götterdämmerung* ('Twilight of the Gods'). The *Ring*'s psychologically and dramatically complex libretto, a work of art in its own right, is combined with an equally complex musical form and structure. In order to sustain such a broad canvas Wagner's musical style became more symphonic in its treatment of themes and motifs, and he increased the mythical, psychological and universal dimension of his libretti. Its story, which Wagner developed from an array of Nordic and Germanic sagas and legends, is based on three main characters – Wotan, king of the Gods, Brünnhilde, his daughter, and Siegfried, her lover and the hero of the entire saga. The story revolves around the possession of a gold ring which promises world dominance to anyone prepared to renounce love. It is an allegorical tale of heroism, greed, betrayal, love and redemption, more than 15 hours in length and composed over as much as 26 years.

The leitmotif ('leading motif'), a theme or motif that denotes a person, object, emotion or event, is the cornerstone of the musical and dramatic development of the *Ring* and Wagner's subsequent works. He used leitmotifs as more than just musical labels; they supported his complex symphonic structure in a truly dramatic manner, acting as reminiscences, anticipating or commenting on events, and even as tools of dramatic irony. The gold in the Rhine, for example, is represented by two chords sung by the Rhinemaidens, and the gold's adventure is, in effect, communicated through these two chords, which themselves decay and become corrupted and tarnished as the fortunes of the gold dwindle.

The pressures of exile eventually broke Wagner and Minna's marriage; Minna had become increasingly unsympathetic to her husband's ambitions. At the same time, Wagner began to have a number of affairs, most famously with Mathilde Wesendonck, whose husband was a wealthy German merchant. When the Wesendoncks met Wagner they were happy to assist the struggling artist since, for them, patronage of the arts was a form of social acceptance. But before long Wagner had fallen madly in love with the wife of his benefactor.

When Wagner met Mathilde he interrupted work on the *Ring* to begin *Tristan und Isolde*, an opera about two lovers whose mutual passion is so intense it can only be consummated in death. The opera was inextricably connected with the writings of Arthur Schopenhauer. Schopenhauer argued that human behaviour is governed by the impulses of the human will, which include ambition, love, hate and – importantly for *Tristan und Isolde* – sexual desire. One possible release from this torment of life is death.

The chromaticism of *Tristan's* music exceeded anything that had gone before. The opera's opening phrase ends on a complex chromatic chord which suggests a resolution that never happens. Wagner promotes this sense of non-resolution throughout the opera, and in this refusal to resolve chromatic dissonance he pushes tonality to its limits. On account of its advanced harmonic language, not to mention the sublime and expressive power of the music itself, *Tristan und Isolde* is one of the most important musical works of the nineteenth century.

In 1858 Wagner fled to Venice after Minna discovered his affair with Mathilde. Other than a brief reconciliation with Minna, he would never see her again. In Venice Wagner completed the second act of *Tristan*. But by the time the opera was completed, Wagner's spirits were exceptionally low. His relationship with Mathilde had ended and, although her husband still supported him financially, he was without the means to realize his musical ambitions. Fortunately, France's Emperor, Napoleon III, commissioned a new production of *Tannhäuser* in Paris in an attempt to build warmer relations with Austria. Wagner saw the opportunity to try, once again, to take Paris by storm, and began to revise *Tannhäuser* for a French performance.

But the revised *Tannhäuser* (1861) was a fiasco, simply because of the anti-Austrian political feelings of a well-organized part of its audience. Wagner was left depressed, suicidal and desperate for success. He took every opportunity to ask for assistance to realize his visionary ambition – the completion and performance of his entire *Ring* cycle. It wasn't long before help was forthcoming. Bavaria's young King Ludwig II had grown up with the world of German myth, and this world came alive for him through Wagner's music. So when, in 1863, in the preface to the published *Ring* poem, Wagner suggested that there must be a prince who could answer his prayers, it was Ludwig who came to the rescue. He became Wagner's greatest patron, and would later enable him to perform the *Ring*. Wagner moved to Munich in 1864 and began plans, with Ludwig, to build an opera house dedicated solely to the performance of his music dramas. He wanted to rebuild the whole city, creating a theatre that would have been the largest opera house ever built. But exorbitant costs ensured that the project never got off the ground.

The conductor in Munich most sympathetic to Wagner's music was Hans von Bülow, who was married to Liszt's daughter Cosima. Cosima soon began a relationship with Wagner which produced a daughter, and the affair became the scandal of Europe. Wagner's relationship with Ludwig was also threatened, because the King's family felt he was spending too much money on the composer. Wagner was therefore exiled, once again, to Switzerland and settled, with Cosima, in a house at Tribschen. Cosima was the perfect partner, combining intellect with adoration for both Wagner and his ideas.

Shortly before they moved to Tribschen Minna died, enabling Wagner to marry Cosima. In the

One of Wagner's greatest supporters was the composer
Franz Liszt whose daughter, Cosima, Wagner married
after a scandalous liaison

more settled atmosphere of his new home he continued the *Ring*, after an astonishing twelve-year gap. He also finished *Die Meistersinger von Nürnberg* ('The Mastersingers of Nuremberg'), his only comic opera, which was more straightforward conceptually than both *Tristan* and the *Ring*. It has been argued that in this period Wagner began to integrate his racial theories into some of the characters of his music dramas.

Beckmesser in *Meistersinger* and the evil dwarf Mime from *Siegfried* are the two most cited examples. Iconography of the time portrayed the Jew as having an inferior body, and one motif in *Meistersinger* is associated specifically with Beckmesser's 'poor perambulation'. In *Siegfried*, at the end of the first act's forging scene, Siegfried's words and music are heroic, in contrast to Mime's musically trivial interjections, representing human degeneration – in the form of the Jew.

'For ordinary people, what defies understanding is the truth that one man could carry in him the totality of that design – could somehow construe, from the first note to the last, a coherent immensity of a complexity which defies analysis.'

———— GEORGE STEINER

In the latter years of his life Wagner's racist views would become more extreme, and his conversations increasingly preoccupied by what he regarded as 'the Jewish problem'. His ideas were undoubtedly barbaric and unacceptable, but not unique to himself: at the end of the nineteenth century, anti-Semitism was, for many nationalists, an inevitable consequence of their views.

In 1869 the strained relationship between Ludwig and Wagner worsened when the King mounted two parts of the *Ring* in Munich without Wagner's consent. But Ludwig continued to idolize the composer, and in the same year, five years after their first meeting, he built a castle that was deliberately modelled on sets from Wagner's operas. But Wagner had little interest in Ludwig's building projects, since ambitions for his own opera house were still not realized. He had various ideas for its location, even wanting to place a stage on Lake Lucerne with the audience on its shore. But this was not practical, and Wagner eventually found his ideal site at Bayreuth.

Bayreuth is the first nineteenth-century opera house designed for the audience to look not at each other, but at the stage. One of the biggest opera houses to have been built, it was ready for the first performances of the complete *Ring* in 1876. It is an amphitheatre, and the orchestra and conductor are hidden from view. A darkened auditorium and a lightened stage forced the audience to concentrate on Wagner's images, for which the 'invisible' orchestra provided the 'soundtrack'. The resulting emphasis on the super-spectacle of the 'total art-work' and its symphonic accompaniment pre-empted the idea of cinema. Indeed, Wagner greatly influenced the earliest film composers, and Max Steiner, who wrote the score for *King Kong*, said that he based his style on Wagner.

Having moved to Bayreuth to oversee the building of his opera house, Wagner worked on his last opera, *Parsifal*. In this opera he returned to the Schopenhauerian themes of renunciation and redemption. The Christ-like Parsifal redeems the heretical Kundry through baptism, and heals the eternal wound of the knight Amfortas. In the prelude to the opera the opening consists of one single line, presented by unusual combinations of instruments. Where Wagner had previously deconstructed harmony, here he was almost deconstructing the sound of the orchestra. He was now at the peak of his musical powers, creating an opera of almost flawless musical realization, with a story of great hidden depths.

Wagner died in Venice on 13 February 1883, aged nearly seventy. His legacy is, both musically and politically, still highly controversial. What is beyond dispute is his greatness. His music aroused more passions, intellectual and emotional, than any music before him – so much so that distinct pro- and anti-Wagnerian 'camps' formed. The German critic, Eduard Hanslick, attacked Wagner's music with that of a younger composer, Johannes Brahms, arguing that Brahms's more 'Classical' compositions made him the true heir to Bach, Mozart and Beethoven. But Wagner had his own direct group of followers. Both Richard Strauss and Claude Debussy found their own musical language and dramatic approach by absorbing Wagner's music. But, most significantly, the tonally ambiguous character of Wagner's last operas was the first step towards the dissolution of tonality in twentieth-century classical music.

Tchaikovsky
and Nationalism

ONE IMPORTANT characteristic of the Romantic period was a growing interest in the past, and many European countries became increasingly aware of their own heritage and national traditions. This new-found identity was also stimulated by political developments in which potentates and sovereigns were forced to give way to more democratic forms of government. Countries under foreign domination began to sever themselves from this stranglehold on their cultural inheritance. Those who were still ruled by foreign powers discovered a fresh individuality in the texts of their national folksongs and the rhythms of their native tongue. Such composers as Mikhail Glinka in Russia and Antonin Dvorak in Bohemia, as well as others in Poland and Hungary, were educated in Italian and German traditions. Now they began to set

Pyotr Ilyich Tchaikovsky – Major Works

Operas
The Voyevoda (1869)
The Snow Maiden (1873)
The Oprichnik (1874)
Vakula the Smith (1876)
Eugene Onegin (1879)
Mazeppa (1884)
The Queen of Spades (1890)

Ballets
Swan Lake (1877)
The Sleeping Beauty (1890)
Nutcracker (1892)

Symphonies
No. 1 'Winter Daydreams' (1866)
No. 2 'Little Russian' (1872)
No. 3 'Polish' (1875)
No. 4 (1878)
Manfred Symphony (1885)
No. 5 (1888)
No. 6 'Pathétique' (1893)

Other orchestral music
Piano Concerto No. 1, b flat (1875)
Violin Concerto (1878)
Francesca de Rimini (1876)
Hamlet (1888)
Romeo and Juliet overture (1869)
1812 overture (1880)
Italian Capriccio (1880)
Orchestral suites

Chamber music
Souvenir de Florence, string sextet (1890)
String quartets
Piano trio

Choral music
Cantatas, services

Piano music
Album for the Young

Miscellaneous songs

music in their native tongue. With the advance of industrialization, cities began to draw large populations away from the farmlands and into the factories. The rural peasant class now joined a growing middle class, who were keen to attend concerts and the opera.

Arts of all forms flourished in Russia, such as the poetry of Pushkin at the beginning of the nineteenth century and the writing of Tolstoy, Chekhov and Dostoyevsky a little later. But it was the composers in Russia who formed the most prominent group of nationalists, and their music drew on the modalities of liturgical chant as well as folksongs. Before the middle of the century Russian music-making had tended to be an amateur activity, confined to the home rather than to the public concert hall or theatre. But with the driving force of the young musician Anton Rubinstein, the opportunities for a wider education in music abounded. The Imperial Russian Music Society was founded in 1859, the St Petersburg Conservatory in 1862 and the Moscow Conservatory in 1866.

The ardent nationalists, however, were largely self-taught. Mikhail

Glinka (1804–57) was the pioneer of a Russian national school; his nationalistic operas and the orchestral work *Kamarinskaya* (1848) had a substantial effect on future Russian music. His 'changing-background' or 'tune-ostinato' technique, in which melodic figures were repeated as a basis on which to build variations, moved the emphasis in composition away from pure musical themes to texture and rhythm. After Glinka there emerged a highly gifted group of composers who were known as 'The Five' – Mily Balakirev, Modest Mussorgsky, Nikolay Rimsky-Korsakov, Alexander Borodin and César Cui. These Slavophile composers wrote strongly 'Russian' works in a highly individual musical language. But Pyotr Ilyich Tchaikovsky, a contemporary of The Five, was the greatest composer to emerge during this vigorously creative and exciting period. He can best be compared with Tolstoy in his conception of his art as being, in some respects, more universal – almost Western – in its conception.

Tchaikovsky was born into a wealthy and musical family in 1840 in the Vyatka province, in a small town called Votkinsk. His father was the factory manager of the local steelworks. As a young child Tchaikovsky heard excerpts from operas by the Italians Bellini and Donizetti – as well as *Don Giovanni* by his later idol Mozart – on the family orchestrion, a kind of barrel organ. In 1848 the family moved to St Petersburg. Here Tchaikovsky was educated from 1850 to 1859 at the School of Jurisprudence, a training academy for the civil service, where juvenile homosexuality was rife. It was during this time, and particularly after his mother's death when he was fourteen, that Tchaikovsky began to write music. But on leaving school he took up a post in the Ministry of Justice until he was twenty-three, at which point he began to study again. Tchaikovsky was one of the first to attend the new St Petersburg Conservatory, where he was taught composition by Anton Rubinstein, its director.

Rubinstein was, artistically and emotionally, the complete opposite of Mily Balakirev, the leader of the now famous group of The Five. Rubinstein was cosmopolitan in his tastes and identified strongly with the standard forms and genres of Western music, such as the concerto and the symphony. Balakirev, however, was vehemently Russian, with more sympathy for picturesque, symphonic poems. Tchaikovsky's early *Characteristic Dances* (1865) has the nationalist music of Glinka at its heart, but the composer was generally more attracted to Rubinstein's ideas and principles. With Tchaikovsky's First Symphony of 1866, and its programmatic title of 'Winter Daydreams', his truer voice is heard – the beginnings of a synthesis between Western traditions and Russian nationalism. The work's more Germanic techniques of development created music immediately different to that of Balakirev and the other nationalists.

> '*Tchaikovsky has the bravery to be open to the bottom of his heart. If we compare him with Beethoven, Beethoven doesn't speak personally to me. Beethoven speaks to humanity. Tchaikovsky doesn't address humanity. He doesn't want to change the world. He wants to talk to everyone individually.*'
> — YURY TEMIRKANOV

Balakirev recognized Tchaikovsky's talent and was keen to make him the sixth member of his group. Tchaikovsky, however, was hundreds of miles away, teaching music theory and harmony at the new conservatory in Moscow founded by Rubinstein's brother Nikolay. Furthermore, his solitary persona, perhaps compounded by sensitivity over his homosexuality, led him to resist the invitation to join Balakirev's circle. But he was undoubtedly influenced by Balakirev, as the nationalist element in his first two symphonies and his early opera *The Voyevoda* (1869) demonstrates. Indeed, Nationalism would reach its fullest expression in his later operas *The Oprichnik* (1874), a grand, historical drama, and *Vakula the Smith* (1876), a fairy-tale fantasy.

The most popular and most beautifully crafted of Tchaikovsky's compositions influenced by Balakirev, and his first masterpiece, is his 'fantasy overture' *Romeo and Juliet* (1869). It was inspired by his passionate infatuation with a young Conservatory student Eduard Zak. ('It seems to me I have never loved anyone so strongly as him,' Tchaikovsky would write fourteen years later.) The work's vivid and resourceful orchestration and its unashamedly emotional themes are typical of later Tchaikovsky. Structurally, the work also made an impact. Tchaikovsky adapted sonata

Nicolay Rubenstein, Tchaikovsky's mentor at the Moscow Conservatory

form to the demands of the story, but used contrasting themes in quite unrelated keys.

His models had been the symphonic poems and descriptive overtures of Liszt and Berlioz, but in the *Romeo and Juliet* overture he used these composers' compositional techniques to more exaggerated and stunning effect. The way Tchaikovsky developed his material is different although related to the traditional Austro-German methods of composition: he used repeated rising phrases

Nazheda von Meck,
Tchaikovsky's
benefactor – a
woman with whom
he corresponded
but never met

that grow in intensity through continually changing harmonies and textures, and emphasized differences in texture as a means of propelling along the musical material. Another shift away from the tradition of Haydn and Beethoven was the idea of closing with a chorale, in a kind of peroration, instead of the standard sonata-form 'recapitulation' and re-statement of ideas. Tchaikovsky employed these programmatic techniques in the more abstract music of his last symphonies.

Tchaikovsky's strongest early work after *Romeo and Juliet* was the First Piano Concerto (1875). His boldness in stating a compelling opening theme in the concerto, without developing the same material later in the movement, brought the work a considerable amount of criticism. But he intended not to state a theme but rather to impose a style where orchestra and soloists are dynamic rivals in emotional intensity. He was unable to secure a performance in Russia, after Nikolay Rubinstein deemed the concerto 'unplayable'. Tchaikovsky refused to change the work, however, and took it to the great Wagner disciple Hans von Bülow. Bülow, who was delighted with the concerto, and who became its dedicatee, gave its première in Boston in 1875 as part of an American tour. The concerto's great popularity is testimony to Tchaikovsky's artistic confidence at this relatively early stage. He had already discovered that the rigorous discipline of conventional musical form was not always necessary in music.

In his ballet *Swan Lake* (first performed in 1877) Tchaikovsky created magical, illustrative music without concern for large-scale structure, and the work does not suffer in any way. Interestingly, Tchaikovsky had attended the first performance of Wagner's *Ring* cycle at Bayreuth the previous year. Its densely structured musical architecture with cleverly interwoven melodic ideas and psychological drama held little fascination for the Russian composer.

Swan Lake is perhaps the most famous ballet ever written, and the *Nutcracker* likewise very popular, but his *Sleeping Beauty* of 1890 is generally taken to be his masterpiece for the ballet. Tchaikovsky was an ideal ballet composer: not only could he evoke atmosphere in purely orchestral terms, but his episodic structures, each with its rhythmic and sometimes symphonic structural formality, were ideally suited to dance.

The theme of fatal love had an obvious attraction for Tchaikovsky, and it recurred in other illustrative pieces such as the symphonic-poem *Francesca da Rimini* (1876), based on Dante's story. For himself, Tchaikovsky began to consider the idea of marriage, hoping it would give him social respectability as well as release from the guilt of his homosexual relationships. In 1877, one of his former pupils, Antonina Milyukova, wrote to him confessing her love. Surprisingly, Tchaikovsky responded and they were married in July 1877. One of the few guests at the wedding was a 23-year-old violinist, Josef Kotek. Tchaikovsky was already infatuated with Kotek and would later write his Violin Concerto for him. The marriage between Antonina and Tchaikovsky quickly became intolerable, and, after three months, they separated.

Tchaikovsky's anguish during this period was recorded in his letters to Nadezhda von Meck, a wealthy widow who had become his benefactor. They never met, but their correspondence over thirteen years was intense and important to both of them. 'The more enamoured I become of you,' she wrote to Tchaikovsky, 'the more acquaintanceship frightens me. In short, I prefer to think of you from a distance, to hear you in your music and to feel at one with you in your work.' Von Meck gave Tchaikovsky both generous financial support and, through her correspondence, offered him the emotional encouragement he desperately needed.

The traumas of his personal life can perhaps be heard in the music of his Fourth Symphony (1878), dedicated to von Meck. The work, particularly its first movement, shows Tchaikovsky to be a supreme master of musical structure and form. He described the dramatic opening idea to von Meck as a 'fate' motif; it appears in all four movements, and by the end of the symphony it has been transformed into a theme. Using a motif as a clear musical thread throughout a symphony was familiar practice in late-nineteenth-century music: Berlioz had adopted it in his *Symphonie fantastique* (1830), and César Franck would do the same in his symphony of 1886. Tchaikovsky used a similar technique in his Fifth Symphony (1888), this time turning the anxious, haunting opening melody into a march of triumph in the last movement.

Tchaikovsky suffered enormously as a result of the failure of his marriage and his sexual disorientation. He spent six months on holiday in western Europe, partly in the company of Kotek, and finished *Eugene Onegin*. The story of this opera, which is both Tchaikovsky's greatest and his best-known, concerns Onegin, who decides to reject the advances of his admirer, Tatyana, but lives to regret his decision. In Europe Tchaikovsky also finished the eternally popular Violin Concerto, and was so impressed by the ballet *Sylvia*, by his contemporary Leo Delibes, that it inspired him when composing *Sleeping Beauty*.

When he returned home in April 1878 Tchaikovsky resigned from the Moscow Conservatory, as he was able to live solely on his annual stipend from von Meck. During this relatively peaceful period Tchaikovsky composed music that was less intense than before: the orchestral suites, the beautiful Serenade for Strings and his more epic operas *The Maid of Orleans* (1879) and *Mazeppa* (1884). He also returned at this time to a plan of Balakirev's to write a symphony based on Byron's *Manfred* (1885). He may readily have identified with the hero of the story – a man doomed to roam in the wilderness to rid himself of unspeakable sins.

Tchaikovsky returned to the theme of doomed fate in his later opera *The Queen of Spades* (1890). Its dramatic concept was very much inspired by one of the most successful operas of the time, Bizet's *Carmen*. The Queen of Spades

'His music is "himself" and the only key is just to understand his character. I think he wrote about his life. He writes a lot about love, because this was one of his tragedies.'

— MAXIM VENGEROV

is about the fascinating character of Hermann, a lonely man devoted both to gambling and to his beloved Liza, who is betrothed to another man; Tchaikovsky identified strongly with both Hermann and Liza. The opera, which effectively recreated the spirit of the eighteenth-century Russia of Catherine the Great, had a triumphant first performance, and after the musical and dramatic success of *Eugene Onegin*, it confirmed Tchaikovsky as Russia's leading opera composer.

A few months later he received a letter from von Meck informing him that because of financial difficulties she was no longer able to support him, and that their correspondence should end. Almost immediately Tchaikovsky composed some of his most arresting and ferocious music by completing his symphonic ballade *The Voyevoda* (largely based on material from his earlier opera of the same name) in just twelve days.

But by then, at the age of fifty, he was enjoying fame throughout Europe and had embarked on a highly successful tour to America, where he was even more popular. In Russia his music was finally receiving the recognition it deserved, but the von Meck rejection had left him devastated and he seemed unable to live at peace with himself. The intriguing Sixth Symphony (1893) confirms Tchaikovsky's melancholic state of existence. Known as the 'Pathétique' (a name suggested by Tchaikovsky's brother Modest), the symphony had a programme, but the composer wished it to remain an enigma to everyone but himself. Tchaikovsky was proudest of this symphony, which he described as the 'most sincere' of his works.

In his earlier Fourth and Fifth Symphonies, the last movements had included peasant jollities and triumphal marches. But here Tchaikovsky ended with a vast slow movement, the subject of which, he said, was death. The movement sinks, despairingly and almost inevitably, towards a deep, pessimistic ending. Once again, Tchaikovsky's determination to express his darkest and most painful feelings led him to create music with a unique and dramatic musical structure. Tchaikovsky often complained, when attempting to write in a true organic manner, of the 'seams' in his music, but these moments actually contributed to a sense of conflict and dramatic confrontation which is the essence of Romanticism in music. It was only after hearing Tchaikovsky's Sixth Symphony that Mahler had the idea of finishing his own Third Symphony with a great Adagio (later repeating the idea in his Ninth Symphony). Tchaikovsky's sophisticated integration of the march and the waltz in his symphonies also had a strong influence on Mahler.

The première of the 'Pathétique' took place on 28 October 1893. A few weeks later Tchaikovsky was buried. Some believe that he accidentally contracted cholera, others that he committed suicide after a 'court of honour' from the School of Jurisprudence ordered him to kill himself because of the disrepute a homosexual affair with a young aristocrat would bring to the school. The controversy over his death continues.

Tchaikovsky was a colossal influence on new generations of composers. His ballets form the backbone of the repertory. His orchestral music, through its original structures and reconciliation of his national folk idiom with Western techniques, revolutionized the whole concept of creative writing. Tchaikovsky demonstrated a talent for manipulating diverse ideas within a musical canvas without, necessarily, the need for traditional thematic development. As well as Mahler, he made a deep impression on such later composers as Rachmaninov and Sibelius.

Partly because of the twentieth-century's obsession with analysis and highly structured forms in all types of 'approved' music – from Schoenberg's atonal experimentalism to the avant garde of Boulez – Tchaikovsky's work has never been given the attention and recognition it deserves. An undisputed master of the 'lyric idea', it has been too readily assumed that what is appealing in his music is shallow. Fortunately, such composers as Igor Stravinsky and Benjamin Britten were astute enough to recognize and appreciate Tchaikovsky as a visionary, particularly in respect of his supreme mastery of orchestration and his highly original methods of creating his own unique sound-world.

Much of Tchaikovsky's music, particularly his lesser-known operas, still needs to be performed – and further research to be undertaken – before an accurate assessment of his oeuvre can be formed (although David Brown's recent study has gone some way towards redressing this problem). What is without question is that Tchaikovsky's music communicates to a huge public more directly and immediately than almost any other composer in the history of Western music. He is as hugely popular today as he was towards the end of his life, and as such he holds a unique place in musical history.

Mahler
and the beginning of Modernism

THE FORM OF THE SYMPHONY has taken different directions in the twentieth century with such composers as Sibelius and Shostakovich, but the intellectual rigour, complexity and influence of Gustav Mahler's work is without equal. His music stands at the end of the Austro-German symphonic tradition, and the last in a line of great composers: Bach, Beethoven, Brahms and, most importantly, Wagner – whose music Mahler first encountered at the Vienna Conservatory, and which he championed throughout his life.

Wagner's music also made a great impression on two other composers who were in Vienna at the same time as Mahler: Hugo Wolf (1860–1903), many of whose songs were influenced by Wagner's rich harmony and declamatory style, and Anton Bruckner (1824–96), who visited Wagner at

GUSTAV MAHLER – MAJOR WORKS

Symphonies	Song cycles
No 1 in D major (1884–8)	Lieder eines fahrenden Gesellen (1884)
No 2 in C minor (!888–94)	Des Knaben Wunderhorn (1888–99)
No 3 in D minor (1895–6)	Kindertotenlieder (1901–4)
No 4 in G major (1899–1900)	Fünf Lieder nach Rückert (1905)
No 5 in C sharp minor (1901–2)	
No 6 in A minor (1903–5)	Cantata
No 7 in B minor (1904–5)	Das klagende Lied (1878–80)
No 8 in E flat major (1906–7)	
No 9 in D major (1909–10)	Song-symphony
No 10 in F sharp major	Das Lied von der Erde (1907–9)
(1910 unfinished)	

Bayreuth before dedicating his third symphony to him. Mahler followed Bruckner in changing the dimensions and even the purpose of the symphony. For Mahler the symphony was 'the world', representing the lure of Nature as well as being a narrative for his personal struggle through life and a search for his own fate and identity.

Gustav Mahler was born on 7 July 1860 in Kalischt, a Bohemian village. He was the second of fourteen children born to Bernhard Mahler, an innkeeper, and his wife Marie. Soon after he was born, the family moved to Iglau (now Jihlava). As a boy Mahler heard everything from military music at the local barracks to folk music at weddings and funerals, including Jewish *klezmer* bands and local musicians in his father's tavern. These sounds, or elements of them, would all contribute to his later eclectic musical style.

The Mahler family was Jewish, but Gustav's musical education began in Iglau's Catholic church as a chorister, and he was taught piano by the choir master. Aged six he wrote his first composition – a polka with, ironically, an introductory funeral march. Throughout Gustav's childhood, many of his brothers and sisters died before reaching maturity. This series of family bereavements juxtaposed with the daily jovial atmosphere in the tavern may well have engendered the contrasts of the tragic and the banal which pervade much of Mahler's later music.

Recognizing his son's musical talent, Bernhard Mahler was astute enough not to force him into the family business. At the age of fifteen Mahler won a place at the Vienna Conservatory. His only surviving student composition is a piano quartet of 1876; it draws on a wide range of other composers' music, particularly Brahms and Schumann. Mahler won several prizes as a piano student, but soon realized that his dream was to compose.

His cantata *Das klagende Lied*, written when he was nineteen, has already a distinctive, highly original style, with assured orchestration; the horn calls, fanfare-like flourishes, off-stage bands and related acoustic effects are typical of his later music. But the work was entered unsuccessfully for the Beethoven Prize in Vienna, and Mahler began to consider, instead, a career as an opera conductor.

He was a remarkably talented conductor and, throughout the 1880s, secured a number of posts at leading opera houses, among them Prague and Budapest. In 1886 he began his first symphony, later called the 'Titan'. Conceived as a symphonic poem, it is, like all Mahler's symphonies, a form of spiritual autobiography. The 'Titan' tells the story of a hero and his journey through life to death; Mahler, in the shadow of Beethoven, saw himself as this Hero. The symphony opens with an eery unison on all the strings, to which are added bird-like interjections in the woodwind as well as sombre horn calls. It is a musical depiction of the creation of the world, before the Hero emerges on the scene. Mahler was always careful to point out that the stories or 'programmes' he offered his audiences were only a vague, helpful guide, and specified that his compositions should always be listened to as 'pure', absolute music.

The First Symphony's première in 1889, while Mahler was director of the Budapest opera, was disastrous. The critics hated it and the audience was baffled. The Mahler biographer Henry Louis De La Grange says that such reactions were not surprising in the case of a highly original symphony 'which included a very strange movement based on the folk-song "Frère Jacques" and which is treated as a grotesque funeral march'. Mahler said that for several days after the performance everybody avoided him in the streets of Budapest, treating him like a madman.

Symphony and song are intertwined throughout Mahler's oeuvre. While working on the First Symphony, he was also composing his first major song-cycle, *Lieder eines fahrenden Gesellen* ('Songs of a Wayfarer');

many of its themes were incorporated into the symphony. The text for the cycle was written by Mahler himself, and it shared the spirit of the folk-text anthology known as *Des Knaben Wunderhorn* ('Youth's Magic Horn'), which Mahler had known since childhood. His later orchestral settings of the *Wunderhorn* poems, in the 1890s, acted, as the Mahler biographer Donald Mitchell has written, 'as a storehouse of invention, symbol and image' for the symphonies he was composing at the same time.

While Mahler's conducting reputation soared, he also gained notoriety for his demanding and arduous rehearsals. He was forced to leave Budapest in 1891 after the appointment of a nationalist Intendant who wished to take artistic control, but was offered another post as Music Director at the Hamburg opera. At this time Mahler decided to devote the summer months to composing, and on the edge of the Lake of the Attersee, at Steinbach, he built his first small hut where he could compose uninterrupted in his own private world. From the summers of his Hamburg period came his Second and Third Symphonies, the largest symphonies he was to write.

In his Second Symphony Mahler, a confirmed agnostic, struggled with the notions of immortality and salvation, questioning the meaning of his own existence. The symphony, which requires enormous resources and which was first performed in 1895, draws on Mahler's *Wunderhorn* settings in its third movement. The grand choral finale (recalling Beethoven's Ninth Symphony in its use of voices) is both uplifting and inspiring; it sets an ode on resurrection by the eighteenth-century German poet Friedrich Klopstock, hence its popular title 'Resurrection'. While at Hamburg Mahler also completed his vast Third Symphony, which has six movements, embracing a great diversity of style and material. Also incorporating music from the *Wunderhorn* songs, and a text from Nietzsche's *Also sprach Zarathustra*, it is a celebration of Nature or, according to its original programme, 'an ascent through the realms of existence'.

In February 1895 Mahler's favourite and musically gifted brother, Otto, committed suicide. Mahler was profoundly shocked. At the same time as this family tragedy, financial restraints at Hamburg were giving Mahler

The Vienna Court Opera, the most prestigious opera house in Europe during Mahler's lifetime

fewer opportunities to achieve his ambitious artistic goals. He now became determined to secure Europe's most prestigious musical post, Director of the Vienna Court Opera. One obstacle stood in his way – he was a Jew. Mahler immediately converted to Catholicism, the official state religion. It was a purely functional move. Although he believed in God the creator, he never belonged to any creed or religion. He used his music almost as a spiritual device to search for his own true belief.

Mahler was appointed to the post of Music Director in Vienna in May 1897, and within a few months he had won great critical acclaim. But he was extremely unpopular with the opera orchestra, many of whom he dismissed. He was both feared and hated but as conductor, stage manager, producer, lighting director, and ruthless dictator he achieved impressive results.

Mahler's Fourth Symphony, which he began in 1899, was the last to be linked to the *Wunderhorn* texts. The words of the last movement come from the *Wunderhorn* song 'Heaven is hung with violins'; and it typifies the spiritual atmosphere of the whole work. Like Beethoven, who interspersed lighter symphonies between those which were more dramatic, Mahler's Fourth is less charged with emotional angst and philosophical perplexities. But here, typically, nostalgia is combined with irony. The symphony's melancholic slow movement is followed by a 'ländler' scherzo, which includes a mistuned solo violin. The

'Mahler broke away from the so-called classical form. It is a symphonic poem, if you want – the creation of the world there in his music.'

—— SIR GEORG SOLTI

symphony begins in one key, and ends in another but, for Mahler, tonality was driven by purely dramatic considerations and symbolic intent. The Fourth Symphony was the first of his compositions to obtain widespread popularity; it was also, at forty-five minutes' duration, his shortest symphony.

Mahler now began to search for a new summer refuge offering the peace and tranquillity of Steinbach, and in 1901 he decided to build his own house in Carinthia, and chose a spot on the edge of the lake of the Wörtersee. In a forest behind the house he had another composing hut built. Here he composed his next four symphonies.

Performances of Mahler's music had met with little critical success. But he was now at the height of his powers, forging ahead with his Fifth Symphony. His triumphant reign at the Court Opera made him both famous and revered in Vienna. Intrigues and machinations at the theatre were recounted daily in the newspapers, and even the city's taxi-drivers pointed him out in the street. But his personal relationships were erratic. His last love affair had been in Hamburg, with a talented young soprano, Anna von Mildenburg, whom he coached to the level of international acclaim.

In November 1901, when he was forty-one, he was introduced to Alma Schindler, an accomplished pianist and composer. Aged twenty-two, she was also one of Vienna's most alluring women and had attracted the attention of the city's most famous artists. Mahler, too, fell under her spell. Within four months of their meeting, they were married in Vienna's Karlskirche. Alma was already three months pregnant with their first child.

This was one of the happiest periods of Mahler's life. But he was also in Vienna at one of the most exciting moments in its cultural and artistic history. An experimental group of artists, led by Gustav Klimt, had broken away from the then conservative Vienna Academy of Arts. They called themselves the 'Sezession' movement. Mahler came into contact with them through Alma and, at the Opera, used a 'sezession' designer, Alfred Roller, to create innovative and successful stagings for his operas. Mahler, who was also pioneering change in opera production, reshaping the orchestra and reinventing the symphony, suddenly found himself with a circle of admiring young musicians who included Schoenberg, Berg, Webern and Alexander von Zemlinsky.

But during this most blissful period of his life, Mahler wrote some of his darkest music. His Fifth, Sixth and Seventh Symphonies, completed over the summers of 1901 to 1905, and without any explicit programme, no longer represented a search for a spiritual existence but were, rather, concerned with the tragedies of human experience. Each of these symphonies begin with a *marche funèbre*, which the conductor Riccardo Chailly describes as 'a kind of unbearable premonition for the tragedies which were following his life'.

The Fifth Symphony reveals the influence of one of Mahler's lifelong idols, J. S. Bach, in the fugal writing and multi-layering of themes and ideas in the second and last movements. The tender, passionate music of the well-known Adagietto is often described as a love-song to Alma; it serves as a moment of reflective calm during the relentless pace of the symphony's complex, enormous structure. The Sixth Symphony offers a psychological study of Mahler's responses to his own impending sense of doom. Some of the most emotionally charged and frightening music Mahler wrote is present in its last movement, notably in the 'three hammer blows of fate' in the lower percussion. Later, intriguingly, Mahler deleted the third hammer blow, probably believing it to be predicting his own death.

The last of the 'trilogy', the Seventh Symphony, includes in its structure two 'Nacht Musik' ('Night Music') movements, around a central Scherzo. Their inner cohesion sets them apart from the other movements, and their evocative atmosphere is unique in Mahler's output. Guitar and mandolin add an idiosyncratic touch to the sensual orchestration of the second 'Nacht Musik'. Its thematic material and exquisite, near-Oriental harmony are skilfully manipulated within a carefully-controlled nocturnal mood.

After their second child was born, in 1904, Alma began to object to Mahler's extensive periods away from home. Even when not composing he would often set off, on his own, in pursuit of Nature. Alma was also unhappy over Mahler composing the *Kindertotenlieder* ('Songs on the Death of Children') based on texts by Friedrich Rückert, who wrote around 400 poems on the deaths of his two children. Alma found Mahler's songs, written between 1901 and 1904, distasteful and, given the presence of their own two daughters, accused him of tempting fate. But he had begun the cycle before his marriage, and strongly identified with Rückert's moving poetry. Tragically, after he completed the song-cycle, his elder daughter died. Mahler went immediately into mourning, leaving Alma to organize the child's funeral and even sell their house at Maiernigg. It was the beginning of a huge rift between the two of them.

Mahler had uncannily predicted his future in his earlier Sixth Symphony by writing the three hammer-blows of fate in the last movement. They now returned to haunt him in the summer of 1907. Within weeks of his daughter's death he was diagnosed with a heart condition. And after a vicious anti-Semitic press campaign accused him of spending too much time away from the Vienna Opera, he was forced to resign from the post.

Mahler's Eighth Symphony had been completed only a few weeks

The composer Arnold Schoenberg was among Mahler's disciples; Schoenberg's radical and revolutionary ideas changed the course of music in the twentieth century.

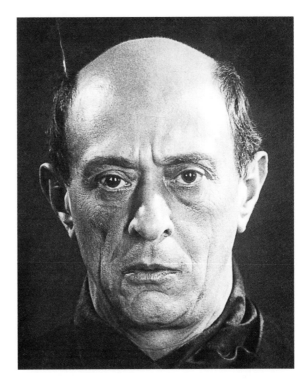

before his daughter died. Its first part is a vast spiritual evocation, making use of the choral hymn 'Veni Creator Spiritus'; the second is a setting of the last part of Goethe's *Faust*. This symphony represents the culmination of two developments in music instigated originally by Beethoven: the enlarged symphonic structure (from Beethoven's 'Eroica'); and the use of human voices in a symphony (as in the finale of Beethoven's Ninth). Mahler's Eighth, popularly called the 'Symphony of a Thousand', has the largest chorus and greatest number of soloists of any symphony.

By this time Mahler had become obsessed with his death. Too superstitious to write his Ninth Symphony (being aware that Beethoven, Schubert and Bruckner all died after their ninth), he instead composed a symphonic song-cycle, *Das Lied von der Erde* ('The Song of the Earth'). It was based on ancient Buddhist texts recently translated from the Chinese. This work no longer refers to birth and resurrection, but seems rather, despite occasional melancholy, as Donald Mitchell says, to indicate resignation to the idea of mortality as 'the music dissolves in a wonderful burst of radiance.'

Mahler was now invited to become the Music Director of the renowned Metropolitan Opera in New York, at a very generous salary. But he arrived there to face yet more political infighting. The manager who had employed him was soon dismissed and his replacement insisted on bringing the young ambitious Italian conductor, Arturo Toscanini, to the Met. It was clear to Mahler that the Met was not big enough for both of them, so he took up an offer to conduct the New York Philharmonic, his first full-time post as conductor of a symphony orchestra.

'By the time the Ninth Symphony is over, you have been truly transported to some other place within your own consciousness; you are forced – whether you want to or not – to reflect on what it is to be a human being and alive.'

— THOMAS HAMPSON

During the summer of 1908, Mahler found a spot in the Tyrol at Tobalch where he could continue composing during the summer months. A third hut was built, and it was here that he composed his last works. Mahler did finally embark on his Ninth Symphony, and it was written during a particularly active period in New York but while he was particularly depressed over the state of his health. Its last movement contains some of Mahler's most moving music, where all sense of pulse and pace disappears in the final bars as the music takes on an ethereal quality. Near the end of this movement Mahler quotes a phrase from his *Kindertotenlieder* as a moving affirmation that his elder daughter is not far from his thoughts.

The final twist of fate in Mahler's life occurred only months before his death. His music was at last beginning to achieve the recognition it deserved, and he was preparing for one of the highlights of his composing career – the première of his massive Eighth Symphony. But the strain of living with Mahler had taken its toll on Alma, who had become an alcoholic. While undergoing treatment at a sanatorium, she began a passionate affair with a young architect, Walter Gropius. Mahler was completely devastated by her infidelity, and blamed himself entirely.

In the gloom of despair, he began his final symphony, the Tenth. Its heart-rending dissonances stretch the bounds of harmony and tonality to their limits. The turmoil of his private life found its expression in the manuscript score, where Mahler in the last bars penned an avowal of love to Alma, and near the very final notes of the symphony he wrote his private name for her, Almschi. The Tenth Symphony was never completed. Mahler died on 18 May 1911.

Gustav Mahler laid the foundations for modernism in music. With his contemporaries Richard Strauss and Arnold Schoenberg, he became aware that the extreme dissonance in his music, used to heighten and intensify emotional expression, was threatening the very fabric of tonality (music governed by a key structure) which stretched back to before the time of J. S. Bach. Mahler anticipated the musical revolution which followed – that of Schoenberg's system of writing music without any key centre at all, where all twelve notes of the scale have equal value.

But, even more far-reaching, Mahler's spatial conceptions of off-stage bands – creating stereophonic effects – as well as his use of small ensembles within larger orchestral structures, anticipated not only Webern and Berg but also the post-war group of composers including Pierre Boulez and Karlheinz Stockhausen. Mahler has been, by far, the most influential composer of the twentieth century.

Puccini
and the Italian operatic tradition

G IACOMO PUCCINI and his stage works represent the final flowering of an Italian operatic tradition which stretched back hundreds of years. Opera in fact began in Italy, where the very first stage productions were lavish entertainments at court. By the seventeenth century the first theatres had begun to appear in Venice. The earliest composers of opera were Peri and Caccini, but the first masterpieces in the genre were written by Claudio Monteverdi (1567–1643). His musical genius originated in his ability to mirror the emotion of his texts, often by using mild dissonance to heighten moments of particular emotional intensity. His successor, Francesco Cavalli (1602–76), developed the idea of *bel canto* (beautiful singing), the writing of vocal lines that would best display a singer's talents. The *bel canto* tradition would dominate Italian

GIACOMO PUCCINI – MAJOR WORKS

Orchestral music	Manon Lescaut (1893)
Preludio sinfonico (1876)	La bohème (1896)
Adagietto for Orchestra (1883)	Tosca (1900)
Capriccio sinfonica (1883)	Madama Butterfly (1904)
Inno di Roma (1919)	La fanciulla del West (1910)
	La rondine (1917)
Operas	Il trittico – Il tabarro, Suor Angelica,
Le villi (1884)	Gianni Schicchi (1918)
Edgar (1892)	Turandot (1926)

opera until the end of the nineteenth century.

Opera during this early Baroque period consisted of a set number of recitatives and arias. In the later Baroque, when the centre of opera shifted from Venice to Naples, Alessandro Scarlatti (1660–1725) used the aria as an opportunity to show off the vocal dexterity of his growing number of virtuoso singers. The operas he and his contemporaries wrote were known as *opera seria*, serious opera. During the Classical period composers began to develop *opera buffa*, comic opera. Domenico Cimarosa's popular *Il matrimonio segreto* was the only opera in history to have received a full encore at its première, in Vienna 1792. The other well-known Italian composer of the period was Giovanni Paisiello, whose *Barbiere di Siviglia* of 1783 was such a well-loved classic that it was considered impertinent for Rossini to set the same story in 1816.

The career of Gioachino Rossini (1792–1868), who bridged the Classical and Romantic eras in opera, was a phenomenal success story. His sparkling *Il barbiere di Siviglia*, based on a story by Beaumarchais, was hugely popular throughout Europe, and admired by Beethoven and, later, Verdi. Rossini's operas had longer scenes, more elaborate musical textures, and made greater use of both chorus and vocal ensembles. The first true Romantic Italian opera composers were Vincenzo Bellini, famous for his exquisitely shaped vocal lines, as in *Norma* (1831), and the more robust Gaetano Donizetti, whose *Lucia di Lammermoor* (1838) demonstrates a masterful handling of vast, complex and dramatic scenes.

Giacomo Puccini's immediate predecessor, Giuseppe Verdi (1813–1901), dominated Italian opera for the entire nineteenth century. In *Rigoletto*

(1851), *La traviata* (1853), *Aida* (1871), *Otello* (1887) and *Falstaff* (1893) Verdi stretched far further the dramatic possibilities of opera, transforming it into a vehicle for expressing the deepest emotions of his often psychologically complex set of characters. His operas also charted the progression of a structure which moved away from set numbers towards a more fluid musical narrative. It was while watching a performance of Verdi's *Aida* in Pisa, when he was seventeen, that Puccini first decided to become a composer.

Giacomo Puccini was born in Lucca, northwest Tuscany, in December 1858. He was the fifth generation of an illustrious family which had provided church composers and organists for the region. His father was a prolific if undistinguished composer who died when Puccini was five. His widow, Albina, despite having little money, was determined that Giacomo, her only male child, should follow in the family tradition. She organized singing and organ lessons for him with his uncle. Puccini attended the Pacini Institute from 1874, and before his experience of Verdi's *Aida*, when he felt that 'a musical window had been opened' for him, he was a dilatory and unenthusiastic pupil. He graduated at the age of twenty-two. His works from his time at the Institute include an orchestral *Preludio sinfonico* and a Motet and Credo of 1878, now known as the *Messa di Gloria*. They are eclectic works which draw on the music of Bellini and Verdi, but some material from the motet and credo would be used in Puccini's first operas.

A grant from Queen Margherita and a generous subsidy from a rich cousin enabled Puccini to enter the Milan Conservatory. There he studied with the renowned teacher Amilcare Ponchielli, whose *La gioconde* (1876) had recently enjoyed enormous success. Puccini's final examination piece was the *Capriccio sinfonica* (1883), in which a critic perceived Puccini to have a specific symphonic talent.

Puccini's symphonic strengths, and his own emotional voice, were to be heard in his first opera, the one-act *Le villi*, also composed in 1883. Illegibility of the score prevented Puccini from winning a competition organized by the publisher Songonzo, but the opera's performance at Milan's Teatro dal Verme impressed Italy's most powerful publisher, Giulio Ricordi. Ricordi was convinced he had found the true successor to Verdi, and provided Puccini with a yearly retainer to compose in comfort. But his

'Matin D'Hiver' by the impressionist painter Alfred Sisley. Impressionism in music, particularly that of the French composer Claude Debussy, was a major influence on Puccini's sound-world.

next opera *Edgar* (1889), based on a tragic story after a book by Alfred de Musset, was a comparative failure. Puccini had laboured with difficulty over this opera (and would continue to be ruthlessly critical of all his works), but saw his way forward through the music of an earlier fellow-student at Milan, Pietro Mascagni. Mascagni's one-act opera *Cavalleria rusticana* of 1889 was typical of the new *verismo* opera; in veristic opera (from *vero*, truth) the subject matter moved away from the historical subjects of the past and was instead based on contemporary life with its full-blooded emotion but, also, its unattractive and sordid elements. Puccini was not, in the true

'[In Puccini] there are human feelings one hundred per cent. There is nothing that cannot be possible in Puccini.'
— JOSE CURA

sense, a veristic composer – since many of his operas are set in exotic locations or have story-lines based on historical figures or events – but the intense emotional style of *verismo* is a feature of Puccini's music that was first heard in his opera *Manon Lescaut* (1893).

Its story of tragic love had been set to music nine years earlier by Jules Massenet. Puccini's opera is the more effective of the two, and there was a huge compositional advance between *Edgar* and *Manon*. Puccini established himself in this work as a true master over his dramatic and musical resources; boundaries between numbers had completely disappeared, and he revealed a sure eye for dramatic effect. Indeed, timing was all-important; in later operas, Puccini would ensure that the curtain at the end of an act fell at the moment of maximum dramatic impact. Influenced by the sexually charged music of *Tristan und Isolde*, Puccini also learned from Wagner the technique of organizing his acts through a highly personal use of musical motifs – without discarding his own distinctive, self-contained melodic invention. The opera, premièred in Turin, was a huge success, and Puccini's fame and fortune were at once assured.

He settled in Torre del Lago, close to Lucca, and could afford to build himself a villa where he could compose undisturbed. He composed slowly, and with difficulty, and was hard to please when it came to libretti. He continually took up titles only to abandon them later, and would often consider many subjects at the same time. Ricordi finally found him two accomplished writers, Luigi Illica and Giuseppe Giacosa, who helped Puccini revise the *Manon* libretto. This collaboration further resulted in *La bohème* (1896), based on Henry Mürger's stories of impoverished Parisian artists, *Scènes de la vie de bohème*. Compared with Puccini's first operas, *Bohème* is a softer and more sentimental work, with a deeply moving final scene similar to that of Verdi's *La traviata*, in which the heroine, finally reconciled with her lover, dies of tuberculosis.

In *Bohème* Puccini was influenced by Debussy in his use of the pentatonic ('five-note') scale – heard if all the black keys of an octave are played on the piano – as the basis for some highly original and striking ideas in his orchestral writing. He was able to dig beneath the surface of the traditional major and minor key system and create a raw but sophisticated and highly expressive sound-world. Although the opera was not fully appreciated at its first performance – the Italian public was unprepared for the constantly-shifting episodes, communicating Mürger's *Scènes* – *La bohème* has become Puccini's most popular opera.

It was while watching Victorien Sardou's play *Tosca* that Puccini came across a dramatic concept that would enhance his stage works and help him communicate even more directly with his audience. He found that he could understand little of the French, but the plot of the play was obvious to him just by watching the action on stage. Puccini's own *Tosca* (1900) – set in reactionary Rome where the cause for freedom is dependent on Napoleon's success – works on this principle of presenting a visually, and aurally, self-evident story. Puccini would use the same technique in his later operas. *Tosca*, his first essay in true veristic opera, played down the political overtones of the play, and Puccini expertly manipulated the emotions of his audience through his fusion of music and drama. It is almost possible to hear the thumbscrews being twisted during a scene in Act Two when the hero is being tortured by the state police. At the end of the first scene, the powerful combination of sexually-charged intrigue and religious piety is typical of Puccini's ability to excite and seduce his audience.

Tosca was reviled by Mahler as being vulgar, although the Austrian composer was initially prepared to conduct Puccini's operas and shared many of his ideals of artistic expression. *Tosca* has most famously been described, on account of its subject matter of sex, sadism and religion, by one eminent American musicologist as 'that shabby little shocker'. However, while the melodramatic excesses of the plot, shorn of sub-plot and historical trimmings, lead to hysterical, overwrought moments, famous arias such as the heartfelt 'E lucevan le stelle' remain within the bounds of pure lyricism. The opera quickly gained a secure place in the international operatic repertoire.

In 1886 Puccini had begun to live with the already married Elvira Gemignani, with whom he had fallen in love years earlier after playing the organ at her wedding. He and Elvira would finally marry in 1904, after her first husband died. But it was always a tempestuous relationship. Elvira had a strong temper, and Puccini was a partner who indulged in serial infidelities. His behaviour became increasingly intolerable to Elvira after he coached the lead female singer for his next opera at their home in Torre del Lago for many months; it was clear to Elvira that the relationship went beyond the professional.

Puccini based this next opera, *Madama Butterfly*, on another box-office success, this time a play by David Belasco. Belasco had made his name as a producer, notable for encouraging natural acting, and using action rather than words to tell the story. *Butterfly* is about a Japanese girl tricked by an American naval officer into marriage, then deserted by him. The opera is set in Japan, and incorporates some real Japanese melodies – Puccini was obsessed with dramatic accuracy, and part of the success of this opera stemmed from his meticulous research into Japanese life and customs, in order to paint the scene correctly. The pentatonic scale is again used, but this time to convey the opera's oriental exoticism.

The duet at the end of Act One of *Madama Butterfly* is among his most intimate love music. Puccini's remarkable sense of theatre, created by

Orientalism was a major influence on turn-of-the-century European culture, but Puccini's 'Madama Butterfly' was modelled on a play which was based on a real-life event.

orchestral colour, harmony and dramatic tension, is at its best in the opera's last scene when Butterfly kills herself. But the work was a fiasco at its première in 1904 (largely as a result of an organized faction in the audience who resented Puccini's success), and he revised the work, cutting certain scenes to give the plot and music more focus. It subsequently became a worldwide favourite, admired by a number of composers including Alban Berg and Leos Janacek, who wrote his own opera *Katya Kabanova* (1921) after attending a number of performances of *Butterfly* in Prague.

Puccini's increasing number of affairs made Elvira more and more jealous and embittered. She eventually drove one of their maidservants, Doria Manfredi, to suicide, after having accused her of an affair with Puccini. An autopsy revealed the girl to have been a virgin. The legal proceedings and enormous public scandal that followed during 1908 and 1909 were a severe strain on Puccini, and delayed work on his next opera.

La fanciulla del West ('The Girl of the Golden West') was based on another play by Belasco, and it had a spectacular première in New York in 1910. *La fanciulla del West* was written on what was, at that time, a fashionable theme – Europe's fascination with America. It is possibly the most underrated of Puccini's operas in terms of its lyrical power and dramatic intensity.

As a pleasure-seeking man who spent most of his wealth on new cars and even a boat, Puccini did not share Verdi's patriotic fervour. He wrote his best music when he could identify personally with the emotional conflict in his characters. So much of his work is intensely sad and reflects his own temperament; despite having an outgoing personality and numerous affairs, he was a lonely and sensitive man. International events tended to pass him by, and he was criticized for showing insufficient patriotism during the First World War. Although he was depressed by the horrors of war, the period was not fruitless for him operatically. *La rondine* ('The Swallow') of 1917 was originally a commission from Vienna but was first performed in Monte Carlo. It is a work light and sentimental in character, frequently employing waltz rhythms. *La rondine* was a success at its première, but it lacks the rich inspiration of his other works and is the least performed of Puccini's mature operas.

'Many composers have been influenced by his general approach to opera – that the music must fit the drama and that, in some respects, the drama comes before the music.'

—— SIR CHARLES MACKERRAS

During this period he also worked on the trio of one-act operas entitled *Il trittico*: *Il tabarro* ('The Cloak'), based on a story by Didier Gold, *Suor Angelica* and the comic *Gianni Schicchi*. This trio of operas – nothing connects one opera to another – is perhaps some of Puccini's most impressive work. Across these operas he divided the melodramatic, sentimental and comic aspects of his talent. *Il tabarro* might be viewed as one of the most powerful of veristic operas, and its sordid tale of murder is effective perhaps because, ironically, Puccini for once composed his music with the minimum emotional indulgence. *Suor Angelica*, a satirical impression of convent life, describes, with unexpected simplicity, a girl's attempt at repentance after an illicit love affair. It was Puccini's favourite of the three operas, but the least well-received. *Gianni Schicchi*, inspired by Verdi's comic masterpiece *Falstaff*, is successful because it is a genuine comic opera. Puccini had, on occasion, used comic sequences to highlight the more painful elements in his stories, but here witty scenes are the backbone of his comic narrative. Since Puccini was so often a slave to dramatic stories and their neurotic personalities, the theatre might be said to have lost one of its potentially most talented composers of comic opera.

Only New York, in the aftermath of the war, possessed the necessary resources to stage the première of *Il trittico*. It was given, in the composer's absence, in December 1918.

Puccini's last opera, *Turandot*, was based on a text by Carlo Gozzi. Its savage drama, set in China, shows him ever expanding his orchestral palette. There is, as in *Butterfly*, exoticism throughout the score, but the treatment of vocal, rhythmic and instrumental textures is quite different. Echoes can be heard in this music of Richard Strauss and of Debussy – whose orchestration Puccini had always admired. His handling of the chorus is superb, the structure of the libretto impeccable, and his characterization, particularly of the slave-girl Liù, at its most poignant. Unfortunately Puccini did not live to complete the opera. He died in Brussels while undergoing treatment for cancer of the throat, undoubtedly as a result of his constant smoking. The final duet of *Turandot* was unfinished.

Turandot is not only the last Italian opera to enter the repertory, but also one of the few twentieth-century operas to be regularly performed. Puccini's mastery of craft, supreme melodic gifts and overwhelming emotional intensity have made his operas the most popular in every major city on the face of the earth. As is the case with Tchaikovsky, his music has been criticized for pandering to popular taste. But his compositions are severely underrated, and further assessment of his work, in an age when little music written for the opera house enjoys even a second production, would be valuable. Puccini, unlike many of his contemporaries, managed to bring the late Romantic idiom into the twentieth century while still maintaining contact with his audience.

COMPOSERS
CHRONOLOGY

1550

Monteverdi 1567-1643

Schütz 1585-1672

1600

Cavalli 1602-1676

Lully 1632-1687

Buxtehude 1637-1707

1650

Purcell 1659-1695

A. Scarlatti 1660-1725

Rameau 1683-1764

Vivaldi 1676-1741

Handel 1685-1759

J. S. BACH 1685-1750

1700

Gluck 1714-1787

J. C. Bach 1735-1782

Haydn 1732-1809

Paisiello 1740-1816

Cimarosa 1749-1801

1750

MOZART 1756-1791

Cherubini 1760-1842

BEETHOVEN 1770-1827

Spohr 1784-1859

Weber 1786-1826

Hummel 1778-1837

Rossini 1792-1868

Meyerbeer 1791-1864

Donizetti 1797-1848

Schubert 1797- 1818

Halévy 1799-1862

1800

Bellini 1801-1835
Glinka 1804-1857

Berlioz 1803-1869
Johann Strauss 1804-1849
Mendelssohn 1809-1847

Chopin 1810-1849
Liszt 1811-1886
Verdi 1813-1901
Offenbach 1819-1880
Bruckner 1824-1896

Schumann 1810-1856

WAGNER 1813-1883
Franck 1822-1890
Smetana 1824-1884

Borodin 1833-1887
Cui 1835-1918
Balakirev 1837-1910
Mussorgsky 1839-1881
TCHAIKOVSKY 1840-1893
Massenet 1842-1912
Rimsky-Korsakov 1844-1908

Brahms 1833-1897
Saint-Saëns 1835-1921
Delibes 1836-1891
Bizet 1838-1875

Dvorak 1841-1904
Grieg 1843-1907
Fauré 1845-1924

1850

Janáček 1854-1928
Leoncavallo 1858-1919
MAHLER 1860-1911
Debussy 1862-1918
Mascagni 1863-1945
Nielsen 1865-1931
Satie 1866-1925
Scriabin 1872-1915
Rachmaninov 1873-1943
Holst 1974-1934

Ravel 1875-1937

Bartók 1881-1945

Varèse 1883-1965
Villa-Lobos 1887-1957

Honegger 1892-1983
Hindemith 1895-1963

Poulenc 1899-1963

Elgar 1857-1934
PUCCINI 1858-1924
Wolf 1860-1903
Delius 1862-1934
Richard Strauss 1864-1949
Sibelius 1865-1957

Vaughan-Wlliams 1872-1958

Ives 1874-1954
Schoenberg 1874-1954
Webern 1883-1945
Stravinsky 1882-1971

Prokofiev 1891-1953
Milhaud 1892-1974

1900

Copland 1900-1990
Tippett 1905-1998

Messiaen 1908-1992

Britten 1913-1976

Walton 1902-1983
Schostakovich 1906-1975
Carter 1908-

Lutoslawski 1913-1994

1925

89

BACH

FURTHER READING

Johann Sebastian Bach Phillip Spitta,
3 vols (Dover 1951)

The Bach Reader Ed. Hans T. David
and Arthur Mendel (WW Norton 1966)

Bach Malcolm Boyd
(Master Muscians, OUP 1983)

Bach: Essays on his Life and Music
Christoph Wolff (Harvard 1991)

RECOMMENDED LISTENING

The Musical Offering
ASMF/Marriner
Ph Duo 442 556-2 (2) [id]

The Art of Fugue BWV 1080
Gustav Leonhardt (harpsichord)
HM/BMG GD 77013 (2) [77013-2-RG]

Brandenburg Concertos BWV 1046-51
Amsterdam Baroque Soloists/Koopman
Erato/Warner Dig 0630 13733-2 (2)

**Violin Concertos (1-2), Double Violin
Concerto** BWV 1041-3
Grumiaux/Krebbers, Les Soloistes
Romandes/Arpad Gerecz
Ph 420 700-2

Orchestral Suites BWV1066-9
English Baroque Soloists/Gardiner
Erato/Warner Dig 4509 99615-2 (2) [id]

(Unaccompanied) Cello Suites
BWV 1007-12
Mstislav Rostropovich
EMI Dig CDS5 55363-2 (2) [id]

**(Unaccompanied) Violin Sonatas
and Partitas** BWV 1001-6
Itzhak Perlman
EMI Dig. CDS7 49483-2 (2) [id]

English Suites BWV 806-11
András Schiff (piano)
Decca Dig 421 640-2 (2) [id]

French Suites BWV 812-17
Ton Koopman (harpsichord)
Erato/Warner Dig 4509 94805-2 [id]

Joanna MacGregor (piano)
Collins Dig 1371-2 [id]

Goldberg Variations BWV 988
Glenn Gould
Sony mono SMK 52594 [id] (1955 recording)

**The Well-Tempered Clavier
Bk 1** BWV 846-69, **Bk 2** BWV 870-93
András Schiff
Decca Dig 414 388-2 (2) [id],
Decca Dig 417 236-2 (2) [id]

Complete Organ Works
Peter Hurford
Decca Analogue/Dig 444 410-2 (17) [id]

Complete Cantatas
Amsterdam Baroque Chorus and
Orchestra/Koopman
Erato/Warner Dig 4509 98536-2 (3) [id],
0630 12598-2 (3), 0630 14336-2,
0630 15562-2, 0630 17578-2

Christmas Oratorio BWV 248
Johnson, Argenta, Von Otter, Blochwitz,
Bär, Monteverdi Ch,
E Bar. Soloists/Gardiner
DG Dig 423 232-2 (2) [id]

Magnificat in D BWV 243
Argenta, Kwella, Kirkby, Brett, Rolfe
Johnson, David Thomas, E Bar
Soloists/Gardiner
Ph. Dig 411 458-2 [id]

Mass in B minor BWV 232
Argenta, Dawson, Fairfield, Knibbs,
Kwella, Hall, Nichols, Chance, Collin,
Stafford, Evans, Milner, Murgatroyd,
Lloyd-Morgan, Varoe,
Monteverdi Choir, E Bar Soloists/Gardiner
DG Dig 415 514-2 [id]

St Matthew Passion BWV 244
Rolfe Johnson, Schmidt, Bonney,
Monoyios, Von Otter, Chance, Crook,
Bär, Hauptman, Monteverdi Ch,
E Bar. Soloists/Gardiner
DG Dig 427 648-2 (3) [id]

MOZART

FURTHER READING

Mozart and the Enlightenment Nicholas Till
(Faber 1992)

Mozart Hildesheimer (Dent 1985)

Mozart: A Life Maynard Solomon
(Hutchinson, 1995)

RECOMMENDED LISTENING

Piano Concertos
Mitsuko Uchida, ECO/Tate
Ph Dig 4382072 (9)

Murray Perahia, ECO
Sony Analogue/Dig SX12K 46441 (12)

Clarinet Concerto in A K 622
Gervase de Peyer, LSO/Maag
Decca 433 727-2 [id]

Flute and Harp Concerto in C K 299
James Galway, Marisa Robles, LSO/Mata
RCA GD 86723 [6723-2-RG]

Violin Concertos
Arthur Grumiaux, LSO/Davis
Ph. Duo 438 323-2 (2) [id]

**Sinfonia Concertante for violin, viola
and orchestra in E flat** K 364
Perlman, Zukerman, Israel PO/Mehta
DG 415 486-2 [id]

Symphonies Nos 29, 35 (Haffner)
Columbia SO, NYPO/Bruno Walter,
Sony mono SMK 64473 [id]

Symphonies Nos 29, 30, 31 (Paris)
Concg O/Harnoncourt
Teldec/Warner Dig 450997486-2

Symphonies Nos 35 (Haffner), 36 (Linz)
Bav RSO/Kubelik
Sony Dig MDK 44647 [id]

Symphonies Nos 36 (Linz), 38 (Prague)
LPO/Beecham
Dutton Lab mono CDEA 5001 [id]

Symphonies No 38, 39
Bav RSO/Kubelik
Sony Dig MDK 44648 [id]

Symphonies Nos 40, 41
VPO/Bernstein
DG Dig 445 548-2 [id]

La Clemenza di Tito
Baker, Minton, Burrows,
Von Stade, Popp, Lloyd, ROHCG Orch
& Ch/Davis
Ph 422 544-2 (2) [id]

Cosi fan Tutte
Schwarzkopf, Ludwig, Steffek, Kraus, Taddei,
Berry, Philharmonia Ch & Orch/Boehm
EMI CMS7 69330-2 (3)
[Ang CDMC 69330]

Don Giovanni
Waechter, Schwarzkopf, Sutherland, Alva,
Frick, Sciutti, Taddei,
Philharmonia Ch & Orch/Giulini
EMI CDS7 47260-8 (3) [Ang CDCC 47260]

Die Entführung aus dem Serail
Orgonasova, Sieden, Olsen, Peper,
Hauptmann, Mineti, Monteverdi Ch,
E Bar. Soloists/Gardiner
DG Dig 435 857-2 (2) [id]

Idomeneo
Rolfe Johnson, Von Otter, McNair,
Martinpelto, Robson, Hauptmann,
Monteverdi Ch, E Bar Soloists/Gardiner
DG Dig 431 674-2 (3) [id]

Mitridate rè di Ponto
Augér, Hollweg, Gruberová, Baltsa,
Cotrubas, Salzburg Mozarteum O/Hager
Ph 422 529-2 (3)

Le nozze di Figaro
Scharinger, Bonney, Margiono, Hampson,
Lang, Moll, Langridge,
Netherlands Op Ch, Concg. O/Harnoncourt
Teldec/Warner Dig 4509 90861-2 (3) [id]

Die Zauberflöte
Mannion, Blochwitz, Dessay, Hagen,
Scharinger, Les Arts Florissants
/Christie
Erato/Warner Dig 063012705-2 (2) [id]

BEETHOVEN

FURTHER READING

Beethoven: The Last Decade Martin Cooper
(London 1970)

Beethoven: A Life Maynard Solomon
(Hutchinson 1985)

The Beethoven Compendium
Ed. Barry Cooper
(Thames & Hudson 1996)

RECOMMENDED LISTENING

Piano Concertos
Wilhelm Kempff, Berlin PO/Van Kempen
DG mono 435 744-2 (3) [id]

Murray Perahia, Concg. O/Haitink
Sony S3K 44575 (3) [id]

Violin Concerto in D Op. 61
Schneiderhan, Berlin PO/Jochum
DG 447 403-2 [id]

Gidon Kremer, COE/Harnoncourt
Teldec/Warner Dig 0630 10015-2 [id]

Triple Concerto in C Op. 56
Oistrakh, Rostropovich, Richter,
Berlin PO/Karajan
EMI CDM7 64744-2 [id]

Symphonies
NBC SO/Toscanini
RCA mono GD 60324 (5)
[60324-2-RG]

Philharmonia/Klemperer
HMV EX 290379-3/9 (6/5)
[Ang AEW 34469]

Berlin PO/Karajan
DG 429 036-2 (5)

COE/Harnoncourt
Teldec/Warner Dig 2292 46452-2 (5) [id]

Cello Sonatas
Jacueline Du Pré, Daniel Barenboim
EMI CMS7 63015-2 (2)

Piano Trios
Ashkenazy, Perlman, Harrell
EMI Dig CDS7 47455-8 (4)

String Quartets
Italian Quartet
Ph 454 062-2 (10) [id]

The Lindsays
ASV CDDDCS 305 (3),
207 (2), 403 (4) [id]

Violin Sonatas
Itzhak Perlman, Vladimir Ashkenazy
Decca 421 453-2 (4), 436 892-2,
436 893-2, 436 894-2, 436 895-2

Piano Sonatas
Schnabel
EMI mono CHS7 63765-2 (8)

Kempff
DG mono 447 966-2 (8) [id]

Goode
Elektra Nonesuch Warner
Dig 7559 79328-2 (10)

Missa Solemnis in D, Op 123
Studer, Norman, Domingo, Moll,
Leipzig R Ch, Swedish R Ch, VPO/Levine
DG Dig 435 770-2 (2)

Fidelio
Ludwig, Vickers, Frick, Berry, Crass,
Philharmonia Ch & O/Klemperer
EMI CDS5 55170-2 (2)

WAGNER

FURTHER READING

The New Grove Wagner John Deathridge
and Carl Dahlhaus (London 1984)

Wagner Barry Millington (Princeton 1984)

Aspects of Wagner Bryan Magee
(London 1988)

RECOMMENDED LISTENING

Der fliegende Holländer
Estes, Balslev, Salminen, Schunk, Bayreuth
Festival Ch & O/Nelsson
Ph Dig 434 599-2 (2)

Lohengrin
Jess Thomas, Grümmer, Fischer-Dieskau,
Ludwig, Frick, Wiener, V State Op
Ch, VPO/Kempe
EMI CDS7 49017-2 (3)

Domingo, Norman, Nimsgern, Randová,
Sotin, Fischer-Dieskau, V State Op
Concert Ch, VPO/Solti
Decca Dig 421053-2 (4) [id]

Die Meistersinger von Nürnberg
Fischer-Dieskau, Ligenza, Lagger, Hermann,
Domingo, Laubenthal, Ludwig,
German Op Ch & O, Berlin/Jochum
DG 415 278-2 (4)

Parsifal
Windgassen, London, Weber, Modl, Uhde,
Van Mill, (1951) Bayreuth Festival
Ch & O/Knappertsbusch
Teldec/Warner mono 9031 76047-2 (4) (id)

Hofmann, Vejzovic, Moll, Van Dam,
Nimsgern, Von Halem, German Op Ch,
BPO/Karajan
DG Dig 413 347-2 (4) [id]

Der Ring des Nibelungen
Nilsson, Windgassen, Flagstad, Fischer-Dieskau,
Hotter, London, Ludwig, Frick, Neidlinger,
Svanholm, Stoltze, Böhme, Hoffgen, Crespin,
Sutherland,King, Watson, Ch & VPO/Solti
Decca 414 100-2 (15) [id]

Tomlinson, Jerusalem, Evans, Elming, Hölle,
Brinkmann, Schreibmayer, Clark,
King, Kang, Von Kannen, Bundshuh, Meier,
Turner,
Bayreuth Festival Ch & O/Barenboim
Teldec/Warner Dig 4509 94194-2 (4),
91185-2 (2), 94193-2 (4), 91186-2 (4)

Suthaus, Mödl, Frantz, Patzak, Neidlinger,
Windgassen, Konetzni, Streich, Jurinac,
Frick, RAI Ch & Rome SO/ Furtwangler
EMI mono CZS7 67123-2 (13)

Tannhäuser
Domingo, Studer, Baltsa, Salminen, Schmidt,
Ch & Phil O/Sinopoli
DG Dig 427 625-2 (3)

Tristan und Isolde
Suthaus, Flagstad, Thebom, Greindl,
Fischer-Dieskau, ROHCG Ch,
Philharmonia O/Furtwängler
EMI mono CDS7 47322-8 (4)

Vickers, Dernesch, Ludwig, Berry,
Ridderbusch, German Op. Ch., Berlin,
BPO/Karajan
EMI CMS7 69319-2 (4)

Mitchinson, Gray, Joll, Wilkens, Folwell,
Welsh Nat. Op. Ch & O/Goodall
Decca 443 682-2 (4)

TCHAIKOVSKY

FURTHER READING

Tchaikovsky: The Quest for the Inner Man
Alexander Poznansky (Schirmer 1993)

**Tchaikovsky: A Biographical
and Critical Study** David Brown,
4 vols (Gollancz Press 1994)

Tchaikovsky's Last Days
Alexander Poznansky (OUP 1996)

Tchaikovsky Anthony Holden
(Bantam Press 1997)

RECOMMENDED LISTENING

Capriccio Italien Op 45
USSR SO/Svetlanov
BMG Melodiya Twofer 74321 34164-2 (2)

Piano Concerto No 1 in B flat min Op 23
Vladimir Horowitz, NBC SO/ Toscanini
RCA mono GD 60321

Mikhail Rudy, Leningrad Phil O/Jansons
CDC 754232

Violin Concerto in D Op 35
Jascha Heifetz, Chicago SO/Reiner
RCA 09026 61495-2

Maxim Vengerov, BPO/Abbado
Teldec, Warner Dig 4509 90881-2

1812 Overture
Minneapolis SO/Dorati
Mercury 434 360-2 [id]

Francesca da Rimini; Hamlet (fantasy
overture) Op 67a
NY Stadium O/Stokowski
Dell'Arte CDDA 9006 [id]

Manfred Symphony Op 58
Oslo PO/Jansons
Chandos Dig CHAN 8535 [id]

The Nutcracker Op. 71
Concg O/Dorati
Ph Duo 444 562-2 [id]

RPO/Ashkenazy
Decca 433 000-2 (2) [id]

**Suites: Nutcracker; Sleeping Beauty;
Swan Lake**
BPO/Rostropovich
DG 449 726-2 [id]

The Sleeping Beauty Op 66
Kirov O/Gergiev
Ph Dig 434 922-2 (3)

Orchestral Suites
USSR SO/Svetlanov
Melodiya/BMG Dig 74321 17099-2,
11700-2 [id]

Romeo and Juliet (fantasy overture)
LOP/Van Kempen
Ph mono 438 311/3-2 (3)

Swan Lake Op. 20
ROHCG O/Ermler
ROH Dig 301/2 [id]

Symphonies
Leningrad PO/Mravinsky
DG 41 9 745-2

Russian Nat O/Pletnev
DG Dig 449 967-2 (5) [id]

Oslo PO/Jansons
Chandos Dig CHAN 8672/8 [id]

**Variations on a rococo theme for cello
and orchestra** Op 33
Mstislav Rostropovich, BPO/Karajan
DG 447 413-2 [id]

Eugene Onegin Freni, Allen, Von Otter,
Schicoff, Berchuladze, Sénéchal, Leipzig R.
Ch, Dresden State O/Levine
DG Dig 423 959-2 (2) [id]

Kubiak, Weikl, Burrows, Reynolds, Ghiarov,
Hamari, Sénéchal, Alldis Ch, ROHCG
O/Solti Decca 417 413-2 (2) [id]

The Queen of Spades (Pique Dame)
Grigorian, Putilin, Chernov, Solodovnikov,
Arkhipova, Gulegina, Borodina,
Kirov Op Ch & O/Gergiev
Ph Dig 438141-2 (3) [id]

MAHLER

FURTHER READING

Mahler: The Early Years Donald Mitchell
(London 1958)

Mahler Michael Kennedy
(Master Musicians, OUP 1974)

Mahler: The Wunderhorn Years
Donald Mitchell (London 1975)

Mahler: The Man and his Music
Egon Gartenberg (Schirmer 1985)

Mahler: Vienna – The Years of Challenge
Henry Louis De La Grange (OUP 1995)

RECOMMENDED LISTENING

Symphonies
London PO/Tennstedt
CZS 5 68059-2 (12)

Chicago SO/Solti
Decca Dig/Analogue 430 804-2 (10)

VPO/Bernstein
DG 435162-2 (13)

Das Lied von der Erde
Dame Janet Baker, James King,
Concg O/Haitink
Ph 432 279-2 [id]

Lieder eines fahrenden Gesellen
Jessye Norman, BPO/Haitink
Ph Dig 426 257-2 [id]

Des Knaben Wunderhorn
Schwarzkopf, Fischer-Dieskau, LSO/Szell
EMI CDC7 47277-2

Das Klagende Lied
Dunn, Baur, Fassbaender, Hollweg, Schmidt,
Düsseldorf State
Musikverein, Berlin RSO/Chailly
Decca Dig 425 719-2 [id]

Kindertotenlieder; Rückert Lieder
Dame Janet Baker, Hallé O/Barbirolli
EMI CDC7 47793-2 [id]

PUCCINI

FURTHER READING

The Operas of Puccini
William Ashbrook (Princeton 1985)

Puccini Mosco Carner
(Duckworth, London 1985)

The Puccini Companion
Ed. William Weaver and Simonetta Puccini
(WW Norton 1994)

RECOMMENDED LISTENING

La Bohème
Tebaldi, Bergonzi, Bastianini, Siepi, Corena,
D'Angelo, St Cecilia Ac Ch & O/Serafin
Decca Double mono 440 233-2 (2) [id]

De los Angeles, Bjoerling, Merrill,
Reardon, Tozzi, Amara,
RCA Victor Ch & O/Beecham
EMI mono CDS7 47235-8 (2)

Freni, Pavarotti, Harwood, Panerai, German,
Ghiarurov Op Ch, Berlin, BPO/Karajan
Decca 421 049-2 (2) [id]

La Fanciulla del West (The Girl of the
Golden West)
Tebaldi, Del Monaco, MacNeil, Tozzi,
St Cecilia Ac, Rome, Ch & O/Capuana
Decca 421 595-2 (2) [id]

Madama Butterfly
Callas, Gedda, Borriello, Danieli, La Scala,
Milan, Ch & O/Karajan
EMI mono CDS7 47959-8 (2) [id]

Scotto, Bergonzi, Di Stasio, Panerai,
De Palma, Rome Op Ch & O/Barbirolli
EMI CMS7 69654-2 (2)

Freni, Carreras, Berganza, Pons,
Amb Op Ch, Philharmonia O/Sinopoli
DG Dig 423 567-2; 447 774-4 (3/2) [id]

Il Tabarro
Leontyne Price, Domingo, Milnes, John
Alldis Ch, New Philharmonia O/Leinsdorf
RCA GD 60865 (2)

PUCCINI continued

Suor Angelica
Popp, Lipovšek, Schiml, Jennings, Bav R Ch,
Munich R O/Patanè
RCA 74321 40575-2

Gianni Schicchi
Panerai, Donath, Seiffert, Bav R Ch,
Munich R O/Patane
RCA Dig 74321 25285-2 [id]

Manon Lescaut
Callas, Di Stefano, Fioravanti, La Scala,
Milan, Ch & O/Serafin
EMI mono CDS5 56301-2 (2)

Freni, Pavarotti, Croft, Taddei, Vargas,
Bartoli, NY Met Op Ch & O/Levine
Decca Dig 440 200-2 (2) [id]

Tosca
Callas, Di Stefano, Gobbi, Calabrese,
La Scala, Milan, Ch and O/de Sabata
EMI mono CDS7 47175-8 (2)

Ricciarelli, Carreras, Raimondi, Corena,
German Op Ch, BPO/Karajan
DG 413 815-2 (2) [id]

Turandot
Callas, Fernandi, Schwarzkopf, Zaccaria,
La Scala, Milan, Ch & O/Serafin
EMI mono CDS5 56307-2 (2) [id]

Sutherland, Pavarotti, Caballé, Pears,
Ghiaurov, Alldis Ch, Wandsworth
School Boys' Ch, LPO/Mehta
Decca 414274-2 (2) [id]

Le Villi
Scotto, Domingo, Nucci, Gobbi,
Amb Op Ch, Nat PO/Maazel
Sony MK 76890

Commissioning Editor: Angie Mason
Author: Kriss Rusmanis
Editor: Ingalo Thomson
Designer: Robert Howells
Picture Researcher: Sarah Pennington
Production Coordinator: Stephen Sillett

Published to accompany the BBC Television series,
Great Composers, Series Executive Producer
Kriss Rusmanis, Winter 1997.

First published in 1998 by BBC Education
Production, White City, 201 Wood Lane
London W12 7TS.

BBC Education is a not-for-profit unit of the BBC.

Typeset in Garamond
Printed by Fairprint Ltd.

ISBN 1 9017 1006 8

For further copies of this booklet, please send a
cheque or postal order for £5.99 per copy to:

Great Composers booklet,
Room 2252
BBC Education Production
201 Wood Lane
London W12 7TS

**Back Cover: Seattle Opera's performance
of Wagner's 'Die Walküre'**